CHOCOLATE OBSESSION

CHOCOLATE OBSESSION

CONFECTIONS AND TREATS TO CREATE AND SAVOR

MICHAEL RECCHIUTI & FRAN GAGE

PHOTOGRAPHS BY MAREN CARUSO

STEWART, TABORI & CHANG
NEW YORK

Text copyright © 2005 Michael Recchiuti and Fran Gage

Photographs copyright © 2005 Maren Caruso

Published in 2005 by
Stewart, Tabori & Chang
115 West 18th Street
New York, NY 10011
www.abramsbooks.com

Library of Congress Cataloging-in-Publication Data
Recchiuti, Michael.
   Chocolate obsession : confections and treats to create and savor / Michael Recchiuti & Fran Gage ;
 photographs by Maren Caruso.
   p. cm.
  Includes bibliographical references.
  ISBN 1-58479-457-7
   1. Cookery (Chocolate) 2. Chocolate desserts. I. Gage, Fran. II. Title.
TX767.C5R34 2005
641.6'374--dc22   2005012701

Designed by The Engine Room
Production Manager Jane Searle

The text of this book was composed in Adobe Caslon, Helvetica Neue and Adobe Woodtype Ornaments.

Printed in Thailand
10 9 8 7 6 5 4 3

Stewart, Tabori & Chang is a subsidiary of

LA MARTINIÈRE
GROUPE

Acknowledgments

We are grateful to many people behind the scenes who helped make this book possible and would like to thank them here.

Richard Callebaut, Gary Guittard, Thalia Hohenthal, Arnu Pless Farm, John Scharffenberger, and Robert Steinberg for their support and sage advice.

Gerald Asher, Doug Fletcher, Peter Granoff, Liz Prueitt, and Lionel Walter for bravely working their way through a variety of wines and spirits to help us decide which ones paired best with chocolate confections.

Mary Risley of Tante Marie's Cooking School and teacher Rachel Leising and her pastry-class students Katie Christ, Chelsea Hertlein, Tanya Krall, Tali Kreindler, Molly Madigan, Melissa McDonald, Samitha Reddy, Erin Roark, Penny Szukalski, Sherry Wong, and Satoshi Yamamoto, who gladly tested recipes and helped us make them better.

Laurent and Erin Katgely for graciously offering their restaurant for a photo shoot, and Sherry Olsen for providing props. Jack Mariani for giving us his grandfather's recipe for green walnut liquor.

The staff at Recchiuti Confections for keeping things running smoothly, even when Michael was elsewhere.

In Paris, Danielle Monteaux, Véronique Rouez, and Chloé Doutre-Roussel for orchestrating the chocolate tasting. Daniel Quirici for linking Michael to Danielle. And the members of *Le Club du Chocolat aux Palais* and the staff at the Hotel Westminster.

Maren Caruso, assisted by Faiza Ali along with Erin Quon and Kim Konecny, for providing beautiful photographs. Leslie Harrington for her production work. The Engine Room, Inc. for the book design. Sharon Silva for her careful editing and Cathy Dorsey for her indexing.

Laura Werlin for the introduction to Leslie Stoker, and Leslie for taking on this book. And Carole Bidnick, our agent, for her steadfast enthusiasm.

Lastly, Michael wants to thank his late grandparents and parents and his siblings for sharing their love of food and for always creating good food. And we both want to thank our respective spouses, Jacky and Sidney, for their unwavering support, especially when Michael disappeared for hours to test recipes and Sidney was crowded out of the kitchen by cupcakes and cookies.

CONTENTS

Acknowledgments — 6

Introduction — 10

All About Chocolate — 13

The Making of Chocolate — 14

The New Chocolates — 15

Choosing Chocolate — 17

Organizing Chocolate Work — 18

Tools and Equipment — 21

A Note on Weights and Measures — 23

A Day at Recchiuti Confections — 24

Dipped Chocolates, Truffles & Molded Chocolates — 27

Instructions for Tempering Chocolate; Dipping and Decorating Chocolates; Making Truffles; and Molding Chocolates — 28

Making Ganache the Professional Way — 40

Infused Ganaches — 42

Ganaches Infused with Tea — 45

Earl Grey Tea Ganache — 46

Jasmine Tea Ganache — 48

Mint Tea Ganache — 50

Other Infused Ganaches — 53

Force Noire Ganache — 54

Lavender Vanilla Ganache — 56

Two-Chocolate Ganache with Cocoa Nib Topping — 58

Lemon Verbena Ganache — 60

Tarragon Ganache with Candied Grapefruit — 62

Cardamom Ganache with Cardamom Nougat — 64

Other Ganaches and Centers — 67

Varietal Chocolate Ganache — 68

Burnt Caramel Base — 70

Burnt Caramel Ganache — 72

Caramelized Ganache with Sesame Nougat — 74

Malt Ganache with Honeycomb Brittle — 76

Fleur de Sel Caramels — 78

Molded Chocolates — 81

Rose Caramel Filling — 82

Kona Coffee Ganache — 84

Ginger Ganache — 86

Star Anise–Pink Peppercorn Ganache — 87

Chocolate and Nut Butter Filling — 89

Michael at the Farmers' Market — 92

Snacks — 95

Graham Crackers — 96

Tahitian Vanilla Bean Marshmallows — 97

S'mores — 98

Fudge Brownies — 99

Rocky Recchiuti Brownies — 101

Classic Ice-Cream Sandwiches — 102

Brownie Ice-Cream Sandwiches — 104

Chocolate Shortbread Cookies with Truffle Cream Filling — 107

Triple-Chocolate Cookies — 109

Chocolate-Dipped Sesame Tuiles — 110

Key Lime Pears — 112

Dried-Fruit Clusters — 113

Candied Citrus Peel — 114

Peanut Butter Pucks — 116

Chocolate-Covered Caramelized Hazelnuts   *117*

Chocolate-Covered Caramelized Cashews   *118*

Whoopie Pies   *120*

Devil's Food Cupcakes with White Chocolate–Espresso Topping   *121*

White Cupcakes with Truffle Cream Topping   *122*

Gingerbread Cupcakes with White Chocolate–Lemon Topping   *124*

Burnt Caramel Pots de Crème   *126*

Double–Dark Chocolate Soufflés   *128*

An American in Paris   *130*

Chocolate Barks   *133*

Cashew-Sesame Dark Chocolate Bark   *134*

Dried-Fruit Dark Chocolate Bark   *135*

Hazelnut, Pumpkin Seed, and Pistachio Dark Chocolate Bark   *136*

Candied Orange Peel Extra-Bitter Chocolate Bark   *137*

Caramelized Peanut Milk Chocolate Bark   *138*

Caramelized Cocoa Nib White Chocolate Bark   *140*

Testing—One, Two, Three   *142*

Chocolate Drinks   *145*

Dark Chocolate Mint Drink   *146*

Dark Varietal Chocolate Drink   *147*

Milk Chocolate with Burnt Caramel Drink   *148*

Milk Chocolate Chai   *150*

Milk Chocolate Malt Drink   *151*

White Chocolate Mocha Drink   *152*

Sauces   *155*

Burnt Caramel Sauce   *156*

Dark Chocolate Orange Sauce   *157*

Dark Chocolate Malt Sauce   *158*

Milk Chocolate Sauce   *158*

Extra-Bitter Chocolate Sauce   *159*

Raspberry White Chocolate Sauce with Thyme   *160*

A Quest for the Best   *162*

Ice Creams   *165*

Burnt Caramel Ice Cream   *166*

Colombian Chocolate Malt Ice Cream   *167*

Meyer Lemon–Buttermilk Ice Cream   *168*

Roasted Banana Ice Cream   *169*

Cocoa Nib Ice Cream with Caramelized Cocoa Nibs   *170*

Vanilla Bean Ice Cream   *172*

A Chocolate-Tasting Party   *175*

Glossary   *182*

Resources   *186*

Bibliography   *191*

Conversion Chart   *192*

Index   *194*

Introduction

This book is our invitation to you into the ethereal world of chocolate, a food with a taste and texture like no other, a food that has intrigued people for centuries. Chocolate's complex versatility leads to many delights. It can be eaten out of hand, each bite breaking with a snap before it melts in the mouth in a surge of pleasure. It can be melted and then blended with cream and butter to make fillings for confections. It can be beaten into cake batters or cookie doughs. It can be added to a simple drink or sauce to elevate it to another level. Indeed, the mere mention of the word chocolate evokes sighs of satisfaction.

Two different paths led to our obsession with chocolate. Michael, whose father's grocery store stocked broccoli rabe, biscotti, and house-made sausages before they were commonplace items, and whose maternal grandmother taught him how to bake at a young age, tasted and used high-quality chocolate for years during a long career as a pastry chef. His love for chocolate confections inspired him to hone his confectionery skills, making chocolates every spare minute, until he was ready to step out on his own. In 1997, he opened Recchiuti Confections with his wife, Jacky, in San Francisco.

Fran, in contrast, grew up in an Irish meat-and-potatoes family with a baking repertoire limited to Christmas cookies that didn't include chocolate. A first trip to France years ago sparked a love affair with French food, and a quest to learn the intricacies of French pastry led her to Gaston Lenôtre's school, outside Paris. She returned home and opened a bakery in San Francisco, using French chocolate for baking and to make a modest line of confections.

Today, there is increased interest in the origins and production of foods, and chocolate is no exception. Some chocolate manufacturers now proudly state the source and variety of cocoa beans that go into their products. Many are making chocolate with less sugar in the European tradition, so the flavor of the superior cocoa beans stands out. At the same time, Americans' tastes in chocolate are changing. Milk chocolate, popularized by Milton Hershey, was once the hands-down favorite in this country. Now people are learning to appreciate bittersweet chocolate as well as less-sweet milk chocolate. These newer, more intense chocolates are the ones we use for all the recipes in this book.

In addition to calling for superior chocolate, our recipes rely on confectionery principles that Michael has developed over the years. One is the use of infusions for flavor. Herbs, spices, and even citrus peels are steeped in cream or other liquids to draw out as much of their essence as possible, whether the recipe is for a confection or an ice cream. Another innovation is the use of deeply caramelized sugar to add intensity to a ganache, a pot de crème, a chocolate drink, a sauce, or an ice cream.

Chocolate's most sublime form, as well as its most intense, is small pieces of candy in which the chocolate is carefully blended with complementary ingredients so that its taste and smoothness remain in the foreground. So we begin with chocolate confection recipes—rich chocolate fillings using infused herbs and spices, rather than the more traditional liquors. The instructions include professional secrets, such as a new way to make ganache, suggestions on organizing chocolate work, and a straightforward tempering technique. Just as the many books about bread have shattered the myth that bread making is difficult, this book will melt away fears about working with chocolate.

We don't stop at confections. The same glorious chocolate is folded into brownies, beaten into cookies and cupcakes, and used to coat lime-infused pears and caramelized nuts. Even something as simple as a hot chocolate drink or a chocolate sauce tastes better when made with superior chocolate.

We invite you to indulge your chocolate obsession and give your palate a treat. Buy some outstanding chocolate and head for your kitchen.

ALL ABOUT CHOCOLATE

The Making of Chocolate

The Mayans and the Aztecs of the New World knew that the pods hanging from particular trees contained seeds, or beans, that produced a taste like no other. The coarse drink they made from them is a far cry from what we know today as chocolate, yet the source is the same.

The cacao tree (Theobroma cacao) on which the pods are found is a tropical plant that grows only within 20 degrees latitude on either side of the equator. Three cacao varieties exist: Criollo, native to Venezuela and the rarest, is highly sought for its delicate flavor; Forastero, a hardier tree that accounts for the majority of the plantings, has a more robust flavor; and Trinitario, a hybrid of the two first grown in Trinidad. The Ivory Coast and Ghana are the prime cocoa-producing countries today, although Venezuela remains an important source for Criollo beans.

The cacao tree (Theobroma cacao) on which the pods are found is a tropical plant that grows only within 20 degrees latitude on either side of the equator.

The pods, which hang directly from the trunks, are harvested by hand and undergo two important steps before they are shipped. First, workers split them open with machetes to reveal the cocoa beans resting in a thick, white pulp. They scrape the beans from the pods, pile them in wooden bins, and leave them to ferment for two to eight days, a crucial step that converts their proteins and sugars into simpler forms, the precursors that will influence the chocolate's final flavor. During fermentation, the beans also absorb the fruity flavors of the pulp. Without fermentation, the resulting chocolate will lack complexity and be too bitter. The fermented beans still contain too much moisture for processing, so the workers carry out the second important step, which calls for spreading the beans on mats and drying them, usually in the sun. Only then are they ready for shipping, sometimes to countries far away.

Once the beans arrive at the chocolate-processing plant, they are roasted, with their size and their moisture content determining the timing and the temperature. Next, a winnower removes the unwanted hulls, leaving pieces of the roasted beans, called nibs. The nibs, composed of about equal parts cocoa solids and cocoa butter, are ground to a paste called chocolate liquor (a confusing term because it contains no alcohol), which is further reduced to the highly minute particles that give chocolate its hallmark smoothness and color.

The final formulation is completed according to proprietary proportions by individual chocolate manufacturers. For dark chocolate, cocoa butter, sugar, vanilla, and often lecithin, an emulsifier, are added to the now-powdery nibs. For milk chocolate, milk solids go in with the other ingredients. White chocolate goes through similar steps, although it lacks chocolate liquor, the essence of the dark chocolates. The final mix goes to the conche, so-called because the original machines resembled

The New Chocolates

shells. Here, the soon-to-be chocolate is kneaded and massaged for several hours, even days, until it has the flavor and texture that the manufacturer wants. Finally, the chocolate is cooled in an exacting way in a machine called a temperer. It is then poured into block molds, cooled completely, and wrapped for shipping.

Some manufacturers, such as El Rey in Venezuela and Guittard in South San Francisco, California, are selecting beans from specific areas in countries that grow superior beans and naming the chocolates for the regions.

Although European manufacturers such as Valrhona, Callebaut, and Bernachon have been making chocolates with high percentages of cocoa liquor and cocoa butter for decades, there has been increased interest in these chocolates in the United States since the mid-1990s. Other manufacturers have rethought their formulas and started making chocolates with less sugar and a greater measure of chocolate liquor, resulting in a more intense taste. Some manufacturers, such as El Rey in Venezuela and Guittard in South San Francisco, California, are selecting beans from specific areas in countries that grow superior beans and naming the chocolates for the regions. Michel Cluizel in France has taken this notion one step further and is making chocolate from beans harvested at a single plantation. The thrust of this approach is to capture a sense of terroir, much as many of the finest winemakers do, highlighting the flavor of specific beans grown in specific places.

These new chocolates typically have percentages, such as 62%, 70%, and the like, listed on the labels. The percentage reflects the amount of chocolate liquor and any added cocoa butter or cocoa solids that the chocolate contains. The remainder of the bar is sugar, a very small amount of vanilla, perhaps some lecithin if the chocolate is dark, and milk solids if it is milk chocolate. Because these chocolates contain less sugar, they are less sweet, allowing the chocolate flavor to dominate.

Even milk chocolate has become more intense. Instead of the 10% minimum chocolate liquor required by the U.S. Food and Drug Administration (FDA), some chocolate makers, including Berkeley, California's Scharffen Berger, El Rey, Guittard, and Valrhona, have increased the chocolate liquor to as high as 45%.

Finally, white chocolate has changed, too. High-end chocolate makers use cocoa butter that isn't deodorized, a practice used by mass-market manufacturers to remove traces of cocoa mass (especially important if it is being extracted from inferior chocolate liquor) and to make the chocolate easier to stabilize. The elimination of this step results in an ivory hue and a better taste. FDA regulations stipulate that white chocolate must contain not less than 20% cocoa butter, 3½% milk fat, and 14% total milk solids.

These new chocolates are bursting with flavor, but their contemporary composition changes the way they react in recipes. Making ganache, the filling for many chocolate confections, is one example. Ganache is a combination of an emulsion and a suspension, like mayonnaise but more complex. Most ganache recipes call for chocolate and cream, in varying proportions, depending on how the ganache will be used. The classic method calls for pouring hot cream over chopped chocolate and then whisking the two together. This usually works with chocolates that contain cocoa liquor in the 50% range. But the new higher-percentage chocolates have more cocoa-solid particles, which absorb more liquid, making it difficult for the cocoa-butter molecules to emulsify. The result is a ganache that looks separated, shiny, and thin. When cooled, the fat particles may even settle on top. This book teaches you how to solve that problem.

The higher-percentage chocolates also act differently when mixed in a batter and baked. All the recipes in this book have been tested with these so-called new chocolates, and the ingredient proportions have been adapted as needed. Here are the chocolates we used to test the recipes:

Dark chocolates in the 62% to 65% range, including Guittard's Etienne collection, Scharffen Berger, and Valrhona, and 70% Valrhona, Scharffen Berger, and Callebaut. Do not use chocolates with percentages in the 50% range.

Milk chocolates in the 40% range, including El Rey, Guittard, Valrhona, and Scharffen Berger.

White chocolates from El Rey, Guittard's Etienne collection, and Callebaut.

Like all chocolates, these new chocolates need proper storage to keep them at their prime. An ideal storage place has a consistent temperature of between 60° and 65°F and humidity below 50%. The chocolates should be tightly wrapped and not exposed to strong odors. Under ideal conditions, dark chocolate will keep for at least a year, and milk and white chocolates for at least six months.

These new chocolates are bursting with flavor, but their contemporary composition changes the way they react in recipes.

CHOOSING CHOCOLATE

Today, you will find a dazzling array of chocolates to choose from for making confections at home. Chocolate manufacturers, in an effort to produce specific flavors, are carefully roasting and conching cocoa beans they blend themselves or using beans from a single plantation. Which one should you choose to make these recipes? One approach is to buy some bars of chocolates that contain the same percentages used to test the recipes for this book and taste them.

But tasting isn't the first step. Instead, begin by unwrapping the chocolates you have chosen and let them come to room temperature. Look at the bars. They should have an unmarred sheen, an indication that they were tempered properly. Next, break a piece from each bar. It should snap cleanly, revealing an interior that is uniformly colored. Pick up the pieces one at a time and rub them between your thumb and forefinger to warm them and release their aroma. Then sniff each piece. Are they different? Can you name any specific aromas?

Now you are ready to taste. Start with the chocolate with the least amount of sugar. (If you have included an unsweetened chocolate, start with it.) Bite off a piece and let it rest on your tongue. As the chocolate melts, it should feel smooth in your mouth and it should slowly release its flavors. There are many descriptors for the taste of good chocolate: fruity, nutty, spicy, even tannic. Try to identify as many as you can. Also, notice how the chocolate taste unfolds. Does it peak quickly and then disappear, or does it build and linger in your mouth? Good chocolate has a cocoa flavor that lasts through the taste and is not dominated by bitterness or sweetness.

Which chocolates are assertive and which are mellow? If you are making a dipped or molded confection, an assertive chocolate needs an equally bold center to match it, while a more delicate filling requires a mellow coating to balance its taste.

In the end, however, the primary consideration is always your own preference. Simply put, select the chocolate with the taste you like best.

Organizing Chocolate Work

Tempered chocolate plays an important role in many of the recipes in this book. It costars with ganache and other fillings to make dipped and molded confections, but it also plays other valuable roles: a basis for barks, a covering for caramelized nuts and dried fruits, a thin finish for Key Lime Pears (page 112) and Chocolate-Dipped Sesame Tuiles (page 110), a coating for Peanut Butter Pucks (page 116), a dipping medium for candied orange peel (page 114) and Fleur de Sel Caramels (page 78).

To make the most of a batch of tempered chocolate, take a tip from the professionals and make your confections in stages: a day for making infusions, a day for other preparations, and a day for finishing. Some of these steps take only minutes; other tasks need more time. The more you work with chocolate, the more adept you will become. This approach lets you divide the work into manageable segments and gives you the freedom to make a range of confections. Unlike bread and pastries, properly stored finished chocolates will keep for at least a couple weeks, so you can have them on hand to give as gifts, serve to dinner guests, or enjoy yourself.

Before you choose recipes and start to work, read the sections on making ganache (page 40), tempering chocolate (page 28), dipping chocolates (page 31), molding chocolates (page 39), and the introductions to infused ganaches (page 42) and molded chocolates (page 81).

The preparation work can proceed at a leisurely pace. Make ganaches and let them rest in the refrigerator overnight or up to two weeks until you are ready for the next step. (The exception is the fillings for molded confections, which should be made the same day the chocolate is tempered.) Make other components ahead, too—toppings for barks, pears for Key Lime Pears (page 112), caramelized nuts—that will be finished with tempered chocolate. Always be mindful of the weather when working with chocolate, however. You need a cool room, ideally 65° to 70°F. If it's a sweltering day and your kitchen isn't air-conditioned, wait for a cooler time. It's also best to work when the air is still, and never near a draft or a heat source.

To the right are four possible schedules, depending on your expertise and ambition. They are intended as general guides; individual recipes give complete instructions. Read each recipe through to insure that you have all the ingredients and understand the flow of events before you begin. A batch of tempered chocolate, made by melting 2 pounds and seeding with 11 ounces, will suffice for each of these schedules.

First Schedule

If you are completely new to chocolate making, start by perfecting ganache recipes and rolling pieces of the ganache into truffles, instead of dipping them in tempered chocolate.

Preparation Day
Make two ganaches that don't require overnight infusion times, such as jasmine tea (page 48), lavender vanilla (page 56), or varietal chocolate (page 68).

Finishing Day
Remove the ganaches from the refrigerator, cut the squares into 1-inch pieces, roll the squares into rounds, and cover with cocoa powder.

Second Schedule

If you are ready to try confections that are finished in tempered chocolate, try two ganaches, such as jasmine tea (page 48) and lavender vanilla (page 56), both of which have short infusion times and are dipped in milk chocolate, and the Caramelized Peanut Milk Chocolate Bark (page 138).

Preparation Day
Make the ganaches and roast and caramelize the peanuts for the bark.

Finishing Day
Remove the squares of ganache from the refrigerator. Coat one side with melted, but untempered, chocolate. Cut each square into 1-inch pieces. Then temper the

chocolate and dip the squares in the tempered chocolate.

For the bark, mix the chocolate with the peanut butter. Pour the mixture into an 8-by-12-inch sheet pan lined with parchment paper and sprinkle the caramelized nuts on top.

Third Schedule

If you are willing to do a little more preparation (some of it only takes minutes), try some ganaches with longer infusion times, such as force noire (page 54), two-chocolate ganache (page 58), tarragon (page 62), or lemon verbena (page 60), and one or two bark recipes that use dark chocolate, such as candied orange peel (page 137), dried fruit (page 135), cashew sesame (page 134), or hazelnut, pumpkin seed, and pistachio (page 136).

First Preparation Day
Choose two ganaches and infuse the cream with the appropriate agents.

Second Preparation Day
Make the ganaches and, if you are making the tarragon ganache or the candied orange peel bark, candy the peel. Roast and caramelize any nuts needed for barks.

Third Preparation Day
If any of the ganaches need curing, such as force noire or two-chocolate ganache, remove them from the refrigerator. Coat one side with melted, but untempered, chocolate.

Cut each square into 1-inch pieces. Cover and return to the refrigerator.

Finishing Day
Temper the chocolate and dip the squares in the tempered chocolate. For the barks, pour the chocolate into 8-by-12-inch sheet pans lined with parchment paper and sprinkle on the toppings.

Fourth Schedule

With the exception of rose caramel (page 82), all of the steps for molded chocolates—tempering the chocolate, lining the molds, making the fillings, and finishing the chocolates—occur on the same day. Choose recipes for molded chocolates that employ the same finishing chocolate, such as rose caramel and ginger (pages 82 and 86), and add caramelized cocoa nib bark (page 140).

Preparation Day
Cut the crystallized ginger and let it dry. Make the cocoa nib topping.

First Finishing Day
Temper the chocolate and line the molds. Make the rose caramel and ginger ganache. Fill the molds. Finish the ginger chocolates.

Second Finishing Day
Temper the chocolate again. Cover the bottoms of the rose caramel molds and make the caramelized cocoa nib bark.

Tools and Equipment

Here is an annotated list, in alphabetical order, of the various tools, pans, and appliances you will need to make the recipes in this book. See Resources for places you can purchase what you do not already have on hand.

Baking Pans

- Straight-sided 8-inch square pan (bottom measurement) for ganaches and brownies

- 8-by-12-inch sheet pan (quarter-sheet) for barks, ice-cream sandwiches, and marshmallows

- 12-by-18-inch sheet pan (half-sheet) for cookies, Graham Crackers (page 96), Whoopie Pies (page 120), and Key Lime Pears (page 112)

Standard muffin cups (2 ½ inch top diameter and 1¼ inches deep) for cupcakes

Cheesecloth for straining cream for infused ganaches

Chocolate dipping forks (nice but not necessary)

Chocolate molds, preferably made of polycarbonate

Coffee grinder (inexpensive) for grinding spices

Copper pot (unlined) for cooking sugar (a good investment if you cook a lot of sugar)

Eye dropper for adding rose geranium oil to Rose Caramel Filling (page 82)

Gold coffee filter for straining Star Anise–Pink Peppercorn Ganache (page 87)

Graters

- Box grater-shredder for preparing chocolate for drinks

- Microplane for zesting citrus peel (handy though any grater with small rasps will work)

Heating pad for keeping tempered chocolate at the correct temperature (optional)

Ice-cream maker

Immersion blender for making ganaches, drinks, and many sauces

Knives

- Chef's knife for chopping chocolate and cutting ganaches

- Fillet knife for making candied citrus peel

Ladles, 6-ounce, for pouring chocolates into molds

Latex gloves (nonpowdered)

Mandoline or V-Slicer for making Key Lime Pears (page 112)

Measuring cups

- 2-cup clear glass pitcher with clearly marked fluid ounces for liquid measures

- 1-quart clear glass pitcher for liquid measures for blending ganaches and drinks

- Metal or heavy-duty plastic cups for dry measures

Nonstick baking liner (not essential if you have parchment paper; Silpat is a good brand)

Oven: All the recipes were tested in a conventional oven. If you are using a convection oven, reduce all temperatures by 25°F and check the item before the stated baking time has elapsed.

Oven mitt to protect hand and arm when caramelizing sugar

Paint brush, small and with natural bristles, for painting chocolate "cups"

Parchment paper

Pizza cutter for cutting Graham Crackers (page 96) (a knife will work, but a pizza cutter is better)

Plastic squirt bottle for filling molds

Plastic wrap

Ruler to mark sizes accurately for ganaches, caramels, cookies, marshmallows, and the like

Saucepans, small and medium

Scale: All the recipes include both volume and weight measures for chocolate, flour, sugar, butter, and the like. Although most American cooks commonly use volume measures, such as 1 cup, 2 cups, and so on, weight is a more accurate measure and thus yields a better outcome. Inexpensive digital scales are readily available.

Sieves (medium size and small) with fine mesh

Spatulas

- Rubber spatulas for mixing and for scraping bowls

- Large offset metal spatula for applying toppings to ganaches

- Small offset metal spatula for smoothing ganaches or batters

- Straight metal spatulas for scraping chocolate from molds

Stand mixer (5 quart)

Stainless-steel bowls (medium size) for melting chocolate, dipping chocolates, molding chocolates

Thermometers

- Candy thermometer

- Instant-read thermometer, preferably digital, with a lower range of 50°F (it's even better to have two)

Transfer sheets for finishing dipped chocolates (optional, but they add a handsome look)

Wire racks for holding chocolate-lined molds, cooling baked goods, and other uses

Wire whisks (medium size) for recipes that call for mixing by hand

Wooden spoons to stir caramelized nuts, burnt caramel, nougats, and brittle (many rubber spatulas will melt and metal spoons get too hot)

A Note on Weights and Measures

All the recipes in this book include both cup measurements and ounce measurements. The ounces are weight measurements, *not* liquid measurements. Avid home bakers and candy makers, as well as professionals, weigh everything, both dry ingredients and liquid ingredients. In the case of small quantities, weight and volume amounts are often equal or nearly equal, so you can measure by either system. However, with dense liquids, such as invert sugar, honey, malt syrup, or melted chocolate, there is a greater discrepancy between weight and volume, so recipes using these liquids state "by weight" after the ounce measurement to remind you that these are dry ounces and not fluid ounces. Weights are not included for very small amounts, such as baking powder or salt, nor are they included for very light ingredients, such as lavender flowers, which weigh fractions of an ounce and would be better expressed in grams.

A Day at Recchiuti Confections

Recchiuti Confections occupies three large rooms next to a freight elevator in an industrial building not far from San Francisco's SBC ballpark, which overlooks the bay. Anyone stepping off the elevator is greeted by the heady aroma of chocolate. One room is the production headquarters, the other a large packing space and small offices, and the third a storage area for packaging materials. Although not climate-controlled, ocean breezes blowing through the west-facing windows cool the rooms, an important factor when working with chocolate.

The production room houses the usual equipment found anywhere food is made, such as refrigerators, an oven, cooktops, sinks, and worktables. But because a chocolate maker needs vats of melted chocolate, some warmed and then cooled to a specific temperature for filling molds or enrobing squares of ganache, machines filled with melted chocolate line the walls. They slowly churn the liquid chocolate, keeping it at a constant temperature. Two enrobers occupy the middle of the room, signifying their importance. These machines, with belts that feed the unctuous centers for candies through a shower of tempered chocolate, then through a long cooling tunnel to set the finish, make the large-scale production of chocolate possible. But they are as mercurial as jilted lovers; they pout, they get angry, and seem to work according to an inner whim.

On a typical day, two workers remove thinly sliced pears from their syrup of Key lime juice and sugar and place them on baking trays to dry in a slow oven. When bone-dry, they will pass through the enrober to receive a paper-thin chocolate coating. Another worker is making ganache for the force noire confections, carefully whisking a large bowl of melted chocolate and cream so it will remain dense, not airy. A fourth is making marshmallows, boiling sugar syrup in a copper cauldron that is an astonishing size, while nearby egg whites mount steadily in a mixer that holds eighty quarts.

Once the pear slices are in the oven, the same two women turn to yet another task: scattering fresh organic tarragon onto trays of an electric dryer. Over the next seventy-two hours, the moisture will be removed from the leaves so that they can lend their intense flavor to the cream used in tarragon ganache.

With the sugar syrup poured into trays where the marshmallows will take shape, the copper cauldron is shifted to another task, this time cooking black currant purée, sugar, and pectin until it is an almost-black purple. After it cools and sets, one of the confectioners will cut it into precise squares of pure fruit esesence, then dust the jiggly pieces with sugar.

The work progresses at a steady pace. Hands are always in motion. When trays and trays of fillings are ready, cut into perfect squares, needing only their final chocolate finish, Michael readies the enrober. The chocolate seems a little hot, but it is thicker than he would like, so he doesn't want to cool it much, which would make it even thicker. He turns his attention to a small, but crucial part of the enrober that needs adjusting. It is the spinning rod that pushes the coated candies onto the belt that sends them through the cooling tunnel. It must be at exactly the right height: too high and the bottoms of the candies aren't coated; too low and the bottoms smear. Michael puts a carpenter's level on it and tweaks its position. He returns to fretting about the temperature of the chocolate. A few test pieces tell him that it isn't tempered yet.

In twenty minutes, the mass of chocolate is a degree cooler, but the chocolates at the end of the tunnel still aren't quite right. He waits. He slows the speed of the belt through the tunnel.

Finally, all the forces line up and perfect chocolates emerge. Once again, Michael is reminded of his mantra: you have to respect the chocolate and give it time—to temper, to set, to crystallize. It can't be hurried.

Dipped Chocolates, Truffles & Molded Chocolates

Instructions for Tempering Chocolate; Dipping and Decorating Chocolates; Making Truffles; and Molding Chocolates

Many recipes in this book require chocolate-tempering expertise, so we start with this critical technique. Mastering tempering opens the door to the world of chocolate confectionery and lets you expand your candy-making skills. Although there are different ways to temper chocolate, we think this one, the "seed" method, is the most accessible, especially for novices. We don't recommend the use of microwave ovens because it is easy to overheat the chocolate, especially with a high-powered appliance.

Tempering Chocolate

Chocolate contains cocoa butter, a complex fat that gives it fluidity and a pleasant mouth-feel. But because of the compound makeup of cocoa butter, you cannot simply melt chocolate and use it as a coating. The confections will lack the sheen and snap that is the hallmark of good chocolate. But if the confectioner heats the chocolate until it melts and then cools it to a precise temperature, the fractions of the cocoa butter will crystallize properly, making a perfect coating for chocolate candies. This process is called tempering.

At Recchiuti Confections, some tempered chocolate is always at the ready for lining molds, slowly churning in machines that keep it at a precise temperature. When it is time to turn individual squares of ganache into chocolate-covered confections, another invaluable machine, the enrober, is primed with chocolate that has been heated until melted and then cooled by the addition of large chunks of chocolate until the mass drops to the correct temperature to produce tempered chocolate.

Although small tempering machines are available, home confectioners can temper chocolate without fancy equipment. Here is how it's done:

- First, make sure you are working on a cool day in a cool space (65° to 70°F) free of drafts and heat. Chop 2 pounds 11 ounces dark chocolate into rough 1-inch pieces. If you are tempering milk chocolate or white chocolate, chop 2 pounds into 1-inch pieces and chop the remaining 11 ounces into 3-inch pieces. Although this is more than home confectioners may need for one session, the large amount stays in temper better than a small quantity and can be reused.

- Put 2 pounds of the chocolate (the 1-inch pieces if working with milk or white chocolate) in a stainless-steel bowl. Put the bowl over—not touching—water heated to a simmer in a saucepan. Do not let any of the water or its rising steam get into the chocolate. Stir occasionally with a wooden spoon until the chocolate melts and registers 115°F on an instant-read thermometer for dark chocolate and 112°F for milk chocolate or white chocolate. Remove the bowl from over the saucepan. Be careful, as the edges of the bowl may be hot.

- Add about 10 ounces of the remaining chopped chocolate, called the seed chocolate, to the bowl and stir occasionally until the temperature drops to 90°F for dark chocolate and 87°F for milk chocolate and white chocolate. Use the additional ounce to get it to the right temperature if needed. Remove all but one of the unmelted chunks, let them cool, wrap them in plastic wrap, and save them for another use. They can be used as you would freshly unwrapped chocolate. The unmelted piece lets you know that the chocolate isn't too hot. If it gets in the way as you work, remove it.

- Now the chocolate is in temper. To test to be sure, use a small offset spatula to spread a thin layer on a piece of parchment paper and then let it cool. If it hardens and looks smooth without streaks, it is in temper. Tempered chocolate has an affinity to stay that way, but if it cools, even by a few degrees, it begins to harden because the cocoa butter starts to crystallize, making it thicker and harder to use. Check the temperature frequently. If it drops, pass the bowl over a gas burner once or twice, or put the bowl into another bowl that has been lined with a heating pad wrapped in plastic, topped with a kitchen towel, and turned on to the low setting (89° to 90°F). It's also important not to heat dark chocolate above 95°F and milk or white chocolate above 90°F, which may cause them to go out of temper. Now the chocolate is ready for dipping centers, lining molds, making barks, or using in other recipes that call for tempered chocolate.

- If you are working with a different amount of chocolate, the general rule is to melt two-thirds and seed with one-third. You can store chocolate left over from tempering in a plastic bag, or you can line a sheet pan with plastic wrap, pour in the chocolate, let it set, and then remove from the pan, wrap airtight, and store in a cool place. Because the chocolate is probably not in perfect temper and therefore not as stable, use it within 2 weeks. It can be used for another tempering session, but do not use it as seed chocolate.

Dipping Chocolates

- On dipping day, remove the ganaches to be dipped from the refrigerator. Unwrap them and put them on a work surface. Using a small offset spatula, apply a very thin coat of melted, but untempered, chocolate to one side of the whole ganache square. This makes the smaller squares that you will dip easier to pick up with a dipping fork. When the chocolate has set, turn the ganache square over. Trim the edges and save the trimmings to remelt for truffles. Using a ruler to guide you, mark a grid of 1-inch squares on the ganache square. Using a thin-bladed chef's knife, cut the ganache into the 1-inch squares along the grid lines, dipping the knife in hot water and wiping it dry before each cut and wiping it clean after each cut. Let the squares sit at room temperature while you temper the chocolate.

- Line the bottom of a sheet pan with parchment paper or with a nonstick baking liner for placing the chocolates once they have been dipped. Slide a dipping fork (or a table fork if you don't have a chocolate dipping fork) under a piece of ganache, lift it, and drop it, chocolate-covered side down, into the tempered chocolate. Push it just under the surface with the fork, and then slide the fork under the piece so that one edge of the ganache is projecting from the tines. (This makes it easier to slide the covered piece off the fork.) To remove excess chocolate from the piece, tap the fork on the edge of the bowl three or four times and then slide the bottom of the fork across the edge of the bowl. Move the fork to an open space on the lined pan. Tilt the fork so that the edge of the ganache touches the pan and smoothly pull the fork out, letting the ganache drop to the pan. Decorate the tops as described below before the chocolate begins to set; you will have about 1 minute. Repeat until you have dipped all the ganache pieces. Let the dipped chocolates sit, uncovered, at room temperature until fully set, at least 1 hour or up to overnight. When handling the finished pieces, wear nonpowdered latex gloves to avoid leaving fingerprints.

- When the chocolate has set, you can trim the excess "feet" from the bottoms with scissors, though it isn't necessary. Michael did this religiously at first and then saw that some fine French chocolates had small feet, so he abandoned the practice. Transfer the chocolates to a smaller pan and cover the pan loosely. Store in an area with a steady temperature of 60° to 70°F; they will keep for up to 2 weeks.

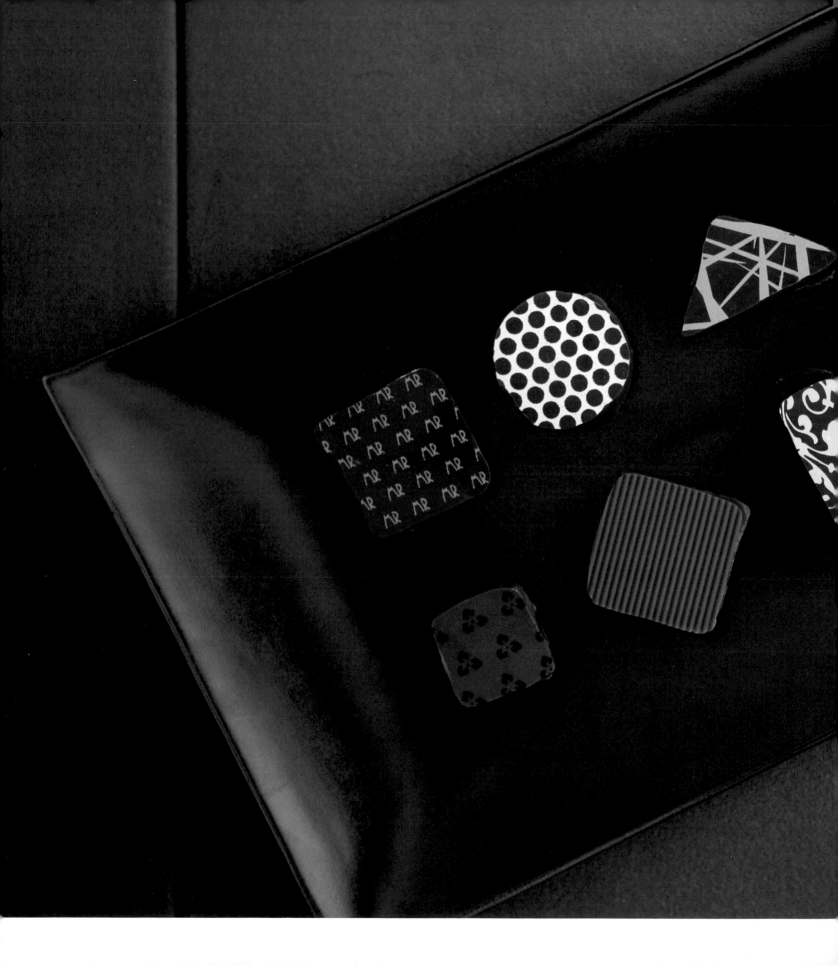

Decorating Dipped Chocolates

Confectioners decorate the tops of finished chocolates so the chocolate lovers who buy them can tell them apart and can anticipate what flavor lies under the thin chocolate coating. Decoration options give you a chance to expand your creative imagination to make the chocolates your own. Then when you proudly present them to your friends, you can match the confections to their favorite tastes, knowing that one swoons for lavender, and another adores anything with ginger. Here are three different techniques for making dipped chocolates look even more finished.

Using acetate squares: A plain acetate square applied to the top of a chocolate gives it an extraordinary sheen. You can touch one side of a square to gold leaf to transfer a speck to the acetate before applying it to the chocolate. You can also purchase transfer sheets of acetate with cocoa butter designs on them (see Resources). Cut the sheets into 1-inch squares and apply them, cocoa butter side down, to the dipped chocolates. Handle the transfers carefully because the designs smudge easily. For a marbled effect, pipe fine lines of a contrasting tempered chocolate onto the acetate squares, then apply them before the lines set. Always apply any acetate square as soon as you have dipped the chocolate, firmly running your finger over the entire square. Leave the squares on at least overnight, or until you plan to serve the chocolates. Remove them before serving.

Using decorative toppings: Sprinkle the sheet pan you've lined with parchment paper or a nonstick baking liner for holding the dipped chocolates with chocolate shavings. After you dip each chocolate, flip it, top side down, onto the shavings. When the chocolate sets, turn each piece right side up onto a piece of parchment paper. Instead of shaved chocolate, you can use cocoa powder, chopped nuts, seeds, plain or caramelized cocoa nibs (see Caramelized Cocoa Nib White Chocolate Bark, page 140), or gold leaf.

Making decorative markings: Let the dipped chocolates sit until they aren't as wet looking, about a minute, and then touch the top of each piece with the tines of a fork or other dipping tool, such as a chocolate loop (if you buy a set of chocolate dipping forks, a loop will probably be included), and pull the tool straight up. Applying squiggles or thin lines of tempered chocolate to the top of each square is another option. Use a parchment–paper cone for piping them onto the squares before the chocolate sets.

Making Truffles

Rolling ganache into truffles is a simpler way to enjoy this smooth confection because no tempered chocolate is involved. Ganache recipes in this book that can be used for making truffles include directions for that option.

- Cut the large ganache square into 1-inch squares as described in Dipping Chocolate, above. Line a sheet pan with parchment paper. Put about ½ cup unsweetened natural cocoa powder in a bowl and dust your palms with cocoa powder. One at a time, pick up a square, roll it into a ball between your palms, and then drop it into the bowl of cocoa powder. After you have made about 6 truffles, shake the bowl to cover the rounds completely. Using a fork, transfer them to the lined pan. Continue rolling until you have used all the ganache.

- Because the truffles are not covered with tempered chocolate, you need to refrigerate them. Transfer them to a bowl or plastic bag that contains enough cocoa powder to prevent them from sticking together. They will keep for up to 2 weeks. Remove them from the refrigerator and put them on a plate about 30 minutes before serving so they are at room temperature.

- For a different look and taste, roll the rounds in finely chopped chocolate, finely chopped nuts, chopped seeds, or cocoa nibs instead of cocoa powder.

- If you have trimmings left from two or three ganache recipes, you can melt them and use them for making truffles. Although the new ganache will be a mélange of flavors, the resulting truffles will be luscious nonetheless. Here's how to turn the trimmings into truffles:

- Line the bottom and sides of an 8-inch square baking pan with plastic wrap. Put the trimmings in a stainless-steel bowl, and set the bowl over a pot of simmering water until the ganache melts completely. It may look separated. Don't heat it higher than 115°F if it is only dark chocolate or 112°F if it contains milk chocolate or white chocolate. Pour the ganache into a clear vessel, such as a 1-quart liquid measuring pitcher. Blend with an immersion blender, using a stirring motion and making sure you reach the bottom of the vessel. The ganache will thicken, become slightly less shiny, and develop a puddinglike consistency. Pour it into the prepared pan and spread it as evenly as possible with a small offset spatula. Allow the ganache to cool at room temperature until it has set and then refrigerate it until it is firm, at least 2 hours or up to overnight. To finish, cut into 1-inch squares, roll into balls, and drop into cocoa powder as described above.

Molding Chocolates

Chocolate molds come in myriad shapes, sizes, and materials, from two-foot-tall egglike ovals to delicate rounds that make bite-sized confections, and from inexpensive clear-plastic shapes found at candy-making supply stores to intricate metal creations. Stiff plaques made of polycarbonate are the best choice because they are indestructible and give the finished chocolates the finest sheen. See Resources for places to buy them. Reserve old scratched molds that you unearth at flea markets, especially in Europe, for use as decorative pieces. Their worn surfaces won't release the chocolates correctly. The chocolate makers in the Recchiuti Confections kitchen employ rat-a-tat-tat shaking machines, bouncing grates, and a cooling tunnel to line molds with chocolate, but you can accomplish the job at home without these devices.

- You can decorate the indentations in molds before you line them with chocolate. To apply gold leaf, cut squares of gold leaf, still attached to the paper, into strips. Put a strip, paper side up, into the indentations and press on the paper so that flecks of gold leaf adhere to the mold. You can also use a parchment–paper cone to pipe dots or squiggles of contrasting tempered chocolate into the indentations, and then either fill them immediately, for a soft contrast, or wait until they set before filling, for a sharp delineation.

- When you are ready to proceed, line a sheet pan with parchment paper or a nonstick baking liner. Put a wire rack in the pan. Place the pan on an even work surface.

- Choose two stainless-steel bowls, one that is at least as wide as the mold (so the chocolate doesn't drip on the work surface as you work) and another that is one size larger. Line the larger bowl with a plastic-wrapped heating pad set on low (89° to 90°F), and lay a kitchen towel over the pad.

- Temper the chocolate in the smaller bowl, and then put the bowl in the heating pad–lined bowl. Using a 6-ounce ladle, fill the indentations in the mold, covering the entire top with chocolate. Drag a straight metal spatula, held at a 45-degree angle, over the open side of the mold to remove the excess chocolate. Tap the side of the mold with the spatula several times to expel air bubbles. Turn the mold over and let the chocolate drain into the bowl, again tapping on the side. When the chocolate stops dripping, scrape the sides and top of the mold with the spatula. Place the mold, open side down, on the rack in the lined pan. Tap it a few more times. Leave the mold at room temperature until the chocolate is almost, but not fully, set, about 15 minutes. Using the metal spatula, scrape any excess chocolate from the top and sides. The chocolate you scrape away should be a firm-butter consistency. (If you wait until the chocolate is completely set, the scraping will fracture the chocolate in the indentations.) Wait until the chocolate in the indentations has set completely, about 15 minutes longer, before filling the molds.

- After you line each mold, stir and check the temperature of the tempered chocolate. If it has cooled below 90°F for dark chocolate or 87°F for white chocolate or milk chocolate, heat it by passing it over a gas burner once or twice, or heat it briefly over a pan of simmering water. Unlike the ganaches used for dipping, the fillings for molded chocolates should be made the same day you make the molds. Let them sit at room temperature until they are needed; they should not be above 85°F. Put the filling in a plastic squirt bottle and fill the indentations to within ⅛ inch of the top. Tap the mold on a work surface to level the filling.

- Refrigerate the molds until the filling has just set, about 20 minutes. Don't chill them too long, or the chocolate will go out of temper when you cover the filling. The exception is the rose caramel (page 82), which must sit overnight at room temperature.

- When the filling has set, once again check the temperature of the tempered chocolate, and then, working with one mold at a time, ladle the chocolate over the filled side of the mold. Drag the spatula, held at a 45-degree angle, over the mold to remove excess chocolate, and then scrape the excess chocolate from the sides of the mold. Let the chocolate set at room temperature for at least 1 hour. The chocolates can remain in the molds, covered with parchment paper, for up to 2 weeks.

- To unmold, rap the molds on a work surface to release the individual chocolates. Loosely cover the chocolates and store in a cool, dry place, not in the refrigerator, for up to 2 weeks. To clean the molds, first scrape as much excess chocolate from the outside of the molds as possible with a pastry scraper. Soak the molds in hot water and squirt them with a stream of water if you have a hose attachment on your sink. Otherwise, wash them with a 100% cotton cloth, using only hot water, no soap. Air-dry the molds. If some moisture is left in the indentations, carefully wipe them dry with a cotton towel to prevent scratches.

Making Ganache the Professional Way

Ganache, a complex emulsion-suspension of chocolate, cream, and butter, is the base for many chocolate confections. Michael believes that three important factors insure a perfect ganache, one that is both smooth on the tongue and retains the essence of the chocolate. These principles apply to every ganache recipe in this book.

The first factor is temperature. Just as the correct temperature maintains chocolate in perfect temper, paying attention to the temperature of the ingredients while making ganache encourages a faultless emulsion, especially when using the higher-percentage chocolates.

Dark chocolate is melted and heated to 115°F (milk and white chocolates to 112°F) and the cream is heated to the same temperature. The butter, very soft (the consistency of hand lotion) but not melted, must be at 75°F. Use an instant-read thermometer to check these temperatures. The temperatures don't lie; they will help you make perfect ganache.

The second consideration is an old confectioners' secret, invert sugar. This is sucrose that is separated into its two simple sugars, glucose and fructose. During the separation process, its crystalline structure changes to a liquid. Adding invert sugar makes for an extraordinarily smooth ganache when using the higher-percentage chocolates. It also stabilizes the suspension and helps the ganache hold its shape, so it can be cut into squares for dipping. Paradoxically, instead of making the ganache sweeter, it brings out the taste of the chocolate. This sugar may separate into its two components, so be sure to stir it before using. If it contains crystals, heat it to melt them. Invert sugar can be found at candy-making supply stores or ordered on the Internet (see Resources).

The third element is the method of mixing. At Recchiuti Confections, the chocolate makers produce large batches of ganache in industrial food processors. A handheld immersion blender is the best tool for the home confectioner—better than whisking by hand or using a food processor. It only takes about a minute to emulsify the ganache. If after a minute it still looks shiny and is thin, keep blending until it loses its shine and develops a pudding-like texture.

Every ganache recipe in this book employs these three critical principles. Follow them and you will produce professional-quality ganache. Then, you can pair the ganaches with tempered chocolate to make dipped or molded confections, or you can roll them into truffles.

Infused Ganaches

Many classic ganache recipes rely on alcohol for flavor. Although Michael occasionally adds alcohol to round out the character of a particular ganache, he prefers herbs, flowers, spices, teas, and, of course, vanilla to complement the chocolate. Many of these pairings may seem unusual, introducing spices usually associated with savory preparations, rather than sweetness. But these ideas bring a new sparkle to the world of chocolate. The quantities of the infusers may seem large—½ cup dried tarragon, for example—in proportion to the rest of the ingredients. But the amounts have been carefully calculated, so don't skimp.

To obtain the maximum amount of flavor, these aromatics are steeped in heated cream, some for only a few minutes, others overnight. Michael seeks out the best sources for his ingredients, buying from local farmers at San Francisco's Ferry Plaza Farmers' Market and drying herbs at his kitchen to insure their freshness.

correct emulsification

incorrect/split

Michael uses floral jasmine, citrusy bergamot, and herbal mint teas to flavor ganaches, all of which he buys from Leaves Pure Teas (see Resources). The teas are carefully blended so that the flavorings and the teas are well balanced—jasmine flowers scent green tea, bergamot oil adds citrus notes to Earl Grey tea, and mint leaves are mixed with other herbs. They only need ten or fifteen minutes of steeping. A longer rest might make the ganache too astringent.

You don't have to use the same brand that Michael uses, but choose high-quality loose tea. If you have a favorite tea, use it instead, but it should not be so strong that it overwhelms the chocolate. The tea flavor should be a whisper in the background.

Here are a few tips on how to get the most out of any infusion you use for a ganache

- After heating the cream with the infusing agent, cover the pan with plastic wrap as it cools. This will trap the volatile oils and make the infusion stronger.

- As noted above, infusing times vary, so follow the instructions carefully. Some infusions, like vanilla, rest overnight in the refrigerator; others, such as the teas, steep for only ten minutes.

- If the infusion has been refrigerated, heat it before straining, not after, to recover more liquid. (This is less important with vanilla infusions, as the small seeds don't trap liquid as much as tarragon or lemon verbena does.)

- The infusing agent will still soak up some liquid, and the amount will vary with the water content and the size of the particles of the agent. Because of this variation, the strained liquid must be adjusted. If there isn't enough liquid, add cream; if there is too much liquid, discard some of it. Each recipe tells you what the strained volume should be.

- When making tea-infused ganaches, sieve the tea leaves before measuring to remove fine particles, and strain the resulting infusion through a cheesecloth-lined sieve. This will prevent a gritty ganache.

- All the tea-infused ganaches (page 45), as well as force noire (page 54), lavender vanilla (page 56), lemon verbena (page 60), varietal chocolate (page 68), and burnt caramel (page 72) ganache squares can be dipped and then decorated with transfer sheets, various toppings, or delicate markings for a particularly attractive finish. See instructions for decorating dipped chocolates (page 33).

GANACHES INFUSED WITH TEA

❖ Earl Grey Tea Ganache ❖

**About 50 dipped squares
or round truffles**

1 cup (8 ounces) heavy whipping cream

⅓ cup plus 1 tablespoon (4 ounces by weight) invert sugar (stir before measuring)

⅓ cup plus 2 tablespoons (1 ounce) Earl Grey tea (shake an ample amount in a fine-mesh sieve to remove any fine pieces before measuring)

9 ounces 65% chocolate, finely chopped

5 tablespoons (2½ ounces) unsalted butter with 82% butterfat, very soft (75°F)

About ¼ cup melted untempered 41% milk chocolate if dipping squares

Tempered 41% milk chocolate for dipping squares, or unsweetened natural cocoa powder for rolling truffles

Earl Grey, Britain's prime minister from 1830 to 1834, liked this tea so much that it was named after him. It is a robust blend of black teas from China and India and bergamot oil, the product of a pear-shaped Mediterranean orange. Michael likes to use a 65% chocolate for this ganache because the stronger 70% chocolate competes with the flavor of the bergamot. It is softer than many of the other ganaches, so after it is cut into squares, it needs an additional day of refrigeration before the squares are dipped or rolled into truffles. The extra time cures the chocolate, enabling it to hold its shape.

Make the ganache

- Line the bottom and sides of an 8-inch square baking pan with plastic wrap.

- Stir the cream and invert sugar together in a medium saucepan. Bring to a boil over medium heat, remove from the heat, and stir the tea into the cream. Cover the top of the pan with plastic wrap and let steep for 15 minutes.

- While the cream is steeping, put the chocolate in a medium stainless-steel bowl and set the bowl over a pot of simmering water. Heat, stirring occasionally, until the chocolate melts and registers 115°F on an instant-read thermometer. Lift the bowl from the pot.

- Strain the cream through a sieve lined with cheesecloth into a 2-cup liquid measure. When the liquid has run through, pick up the cheesecloth and squeeze the remaining drops into the sieve. If necessary, add cream or discard some of the liquid to bring the volume to 10 ounces. Check to make sure the temperature is at 115°F and adjust if necessary.

- Pour the chocolate and cream into a 1-quart clear vessel. Blend with an immersion blender using a stirring motion and making sure you reach the bottom of the vessel. The ganache will thicken, become slightly less shiny, and develop a puddinglike consistency. Add the butter and incorporate it with the immersion blender.

- Pour the ganache into the lined pan. Spread it as evenly as possible with a small offset spatula. Allow the ganache to cool at room temperature until it has set, 2 to 4 hours. Cover the pan with plastic wrap and refrigerate until you are ready to dip squares or roll truffles.

Dip the ganache squares in chocolate or make truffles

- See instructions for tempering chocolate (page 28), dipping chocolates (page 31), and making truffles (page 37).

- Lift the square of ganache from the pan, turn it over onto a work surface, and remove the plastic wrap. If you are dipping squares, apply a thin coat of melted untempered (112°F) 41% milk chocolate to one side of the ganache square with a small offset spatula. (If you are making truffles, don't apply the chocolate coating.) Let the chocolate harden. Turn the ganache square over and trim the edges. Cut the ganache into 1-inch squares with a knife dipped in hot water and wiped dry before each cut and wiped clean after each cut. Separate the pieces, put them on a sheet pan lined with parchment paper, and cover them with plastic wrap. Refrigerate the squares for 1 day before dipping them in tempered chocolate or rolling them into truffles.

- The next day, remove the squares from the refrigerator. If you are dipping squares, temper the chocolate and then dip the squares. Store the dipped chocolates in a cool, dry place, not in the refrigerator.

- If you are making truffles, dust your palms with cocoa powder, roll the ganache squares into balls, and then coat with cocoa powder. Place the truffles in a bowl or plastic bag that contains enough cocoa powder to keep them from sticking together. Store in the refrigerator, but remove them 30 minutes before serving.

✤ Jasmine Tea Ganache ✤

**About 50 dipped squares
or round truffles**

¾ cup plus 2 tablespoons (7 ounces)
heavy whipping cream

⅓ cup (3½ ounces by weight) invert
sugar (stir before measuring)

¼ cup (½ ounce) jasmine tea (shake
an ample amount in a fine-mesh
sieve to remove any fine pieces before measuring)

9¾ ounces 70% chocolate, finely
chopped

5 tablespoons (2½ ounces) unsalted
butter with 82% butterfat, very soft
(75°F)

About ¼ cup melted untempered
41% milk chocolate if dipping
squares

Tempered 41% milk chocolate for
dipping squares, or unsweetened
natural cocoa powder for rolling
truffles

The floral tones of jasmine tea are a good match for the 70% chocolate, while the thin coating of milk chocolate rounds out the taste. This ganache is softer than many of the other ganaches, so after it is cut into squares, it needs an additional day of refrigeration before the squares are dipped or rolled into truffles. The extra time cures the chocolate, enabling it to hold its shape.

Make the ganache

- Line the bottom and sides of an 8-inch square baking pan with plastic wrap.

- Stir the cream and invert sugar together in a medium saucepan. Bring to a boil over medium heat, remove from the heat, and stir the tea into the cream. Cover the top of the pan with plastic wrap and let steep for 15 minutes.

- While the cream is steeping, put the chocolate in a medium stainless-steel bowl and set the bowl over a pot of simmering water. Heat, stirring occasionally, until the chocolate melts and registers 115°F on an instant-read thermometer. Lift the bowl from the pot.

- Strain the cream through a sieve lined with cheesecloth into a 2-cup liquid measure. When the liquid has run through, pick up the cheesecloth and squeeze the remaining drops into the sieve. If necessary, add cream or discard some of the liquid to bring the volume to 9¼ ounces. Check to make sure the temperature is at 115°F and adjust if necessary.

- Pour the chocolate and infused cream into a 1-quart clear vessel. Blend with an immersion blender using a stirring motion and making sure you reach the bottom of the vessel. The ganache will thicken, become slightly less shiny, and develop a pudding-like consistency Add the butter and incorporate it with the immersion blender.

- Pour the ganache into the lined pan. Spread it as evenly as possible with a small offset spatula. Allow the ganache to cool at room temperature until it has set, 2 to 4 hours. Cover the pan with plastic wrap and refrigerate until you are ready to dip squares or roll truffles.

Dip the ganache squares in chocolate or make truffles

- See instructions for tempering chocolate (page 28), dipping chocolates (page 31), and making truffles (page 37).

- Lift the square of ganache from the pan, turn it over onto a work surface, and remove the plastic wrap. If you are dipping squares, apply a thin coat of melted untempered (112°F) milk chocolate to one side of the ganache square with a small offset spatula. (If you are making truffles, don't apply the chocolate coating.) Let the chocolate harden. Turn the ganache square over and trim the edges. Cut the ganache into 1-inch squares with a knife dipped in hot water and wiped dry before each cut and wiped clean after each cut. Separate the pieces, put them on a sheet pan lined with parchment paper, and cover them with plastic wrap. Refrigerate the squares for 1 more day before dipping them in tempered chocolate or rolling them into truffles.

- The next day, remove the squares from the refrigerator. If you are dipping squares, temper the chocolate and then dip the squares. Store the dipped chocolates in a cool, dry place, not in the refrigerator.

- If you are making truffles, dust your palms with cocoa powder, roll the ganache squares into balls, and then coat with cocoa powder. Place the truffles in a bowl or plastic bag that contains enough cocoa powder to keep them from sticking together. Store in the refrigerator, but remove them 30 minutes before serving.

❖ Mint Tea Ganache ❖

**About 50 dipped squares
or round truffles**

1½ cups (12 ounces) heavy whipping
cream

⅓ cup (3½ ounces by weight) invert
sugar (stir before measuring)

½ cup (1¼ ounces) mint tea (shake
an ample amount in a fine-mesh
sieve to remove any fine pieces before measuring)

7¾ ounces 70% chocolate, finely
chopped

4 tablespoons (2 ounces) unsalted
butter with 82% butterfat, very soft
(75°F)

About ¼ cup melted untempered
65% chocolate if dipping squares

Tempered 65% chocolate for dipping
squares, or unsweetened natural
cocoa powder for rolling truffles

Rather than using an herbal mint tea for this ganache, use a tea that is a mixture of green tea leaves and dried mint. It will result in a confection with a subtle, not-too-minty flavor. This combination is more assertive than what is used in our other tea-infused ganaches, so dark chocolate is used both for the ganache and for dipping.

Because it is softer than many of the others, this ganache needs an additional day of refrigeration after it is cut into small squares before the squares are dipped or rolled into truffles. The extra time cures the chocolate, enabling it to hold its shape.

Make the ganache

- Line the bottom and sides of an 8-inch square baking pan with plastic wrap.

- Stir the cream and invert sugar together in a medium saucepan. Bring to a boil over medium heat, remove from the heat, and stir the tea into the cream. Cover the top of the pan with plastic wrap and let steep for 15 minutes.

- While the cream is steeping, put the chocolate in a medium stainless-steel bowl and set the bowl over a pot of simmering water. Heat, stirring occasionally, until the chocolate melts and registers 115°F on an instant-read thermometer. Lift the bowl from the pot.

- Strain the cream through a sieve lined with cheesecloth into a 2-cup liquid measure. When the liquid has run through, pick up the cheesecloth and squeeze the remaining drops into the sieve. If necessary, add cream or discard some of the liquid to bring the volume to 10¼ ounces. Check to make sure the temperature is at 115°F and adjust if necessary.

- Pour the chocolate and infused cream into a 1-quart clear vessel. Blend with an immersion blender using a stirring motion and making sure you reach the bottom of the vessel. The ganache will thicken, become slightly less shiny, and develop a pudding-like consistency Add the butter and incorporate it with the immersion blender.

- Pour the ganache into the lined pan. Spread it as evenly as possible with a small offset spatula. Allow the ganache to cool at room temperature until it has set, 2 to 4 hours. Cover the pan with plastic wrap and refrigerate until you are ready to dip squares or roll truffles.

Dip the ganache squares in chocolate or make truffles

- See instructions for tempering chocolate (page 28), dipping chocolates (page 31), and making truffles (page 37).

- Lift the square of ganache from the pan, turn it over onto a work surface, and remove the plastic wrap. If you are dipping squares, apply a thin coat of melted untempered (115°F) 65% chocolate to one side of the ganache square with a small offset spatula. (If you are making truffles, don't apply the chocolate coating.) Let the chocolate harden. Turn the ganache square over and trim the edges. Cut the ganache into 1-inch squares with a knife dipped in hot water and wiped dry before each cut and wiped clean after each cut. Separate the pieces, put them on a sheet pan lined with parchment paper, and cover them with plastic wrap. Refrigerate the squares for 1 more day before dipping them in tempered chocolate or rolling them into truffles.

- The next day, remove the squares from the refrigerator. If you are dipping squares, temper the chocolate and then dip the squares. Store the dipped chocolates in a cool, dry place, not in the refrigerator.

- If you are making truffles, dust your palms with cocoa powder, roll the ganache squares into balls, and then coat with cocoa powder. Place the truffles in a bowl or plastic bag that contains enough cocoa powder to keep them from sticking together. Store in the refrigerator, but remove them 30 minutes before serving.

Other Infused Ganaches

❖ Force Noire Ganache ❖

About 50 dipped squares or round truffles

½ cup (4 ounces) heavy whipping cream

¼ cup plus 3 tablespoons (4½ ounces by weight) invert sugar (stir before measuring)

1 Tahitian vanilla bean, split horizontally

12 ounces 61% to 70% chocolate, finely chopped

3 tablespoons (1½ ounces) unsalted butter with 82% butterfat, very soft (75°F)

About ¼ cup melted untempered 61% to 70% chocolate if dipping squares

Tempered 61% to 70% chocolate for dipping squares, or unsweetened natural cocoa powder for rolling truffles

The dominant taste in this ganache is the chocolate. Use your favorite dark chocolate with an intense flavor. The seeds from a Tahitian vanilla bean, along with the split bean, are heated in the cream and then steeped overnight in the refrigerator to draw out as much flavor as possible. The floral tones of the vanilla complement the richness of the chocolate.

Make the ganache

- Stir the cream and invert sugar together in a medium saucepan. Scrape the vanilla seeds from the bean into the pan and then add the bean. Bring to a boil over medium heat, remove from the heat, and cover the top of the pan with plastic wrap. When the cream has cooled to room temperature, transfer it to a bowl, cover, and refrigerate overnight.

- Line the bottom and sides of an 8-inch square baking pan with plastic wrap.

- Put the chocolate in a medium stainless-steel bowl and set the bowl over a pot of simmering water. Heat, stirring occasionally, until the chocolate melts and registers 115°F on an instant-read thermometer. Lift the bowl from the pot.

- When the chocolate is almost at 115°F, remove the cream from the refrigerator. Strain it through a fine-mesh sieve into a small saucepan and heat it to 115°F, stirring occasionally.

- Pour the chocolate and the cream into a 1-quart clear vessel. Blend with an immersion blender using a stirring motion and making sure you reach the bottom of the vessel. The ganache will thicken, become slightly less shiny, and develop a pudding-like consistency. Add the butter and incorporate it with the immersion blender.

- Pour the ganache into the lined pan. Spread it as evenly as possible with a small offset spatula. Allow the ganache to cool at room temperature until it has set, 2 to 4 hours. Cover the pan with plastic wrap and refrigerate until you are ready to dip squares or roll truffles.

Dip the ganache squares in chocolate or make truffles

- See instructions for tempering chocolate (page 28), dipping chocolates (page 31), and making truffles (page 37).

- Lift the square of ganache from the pan, turn it over onto a work surface, and remove the plastic wrap. If you are dipping squares, apply a thin coat of melted untempered (115°F) 61% to 70% chocolate to one side of the ganache square with a small offset spatula. (If you are making truffles, don't apply the chocolate coating.) Let the chocolate harden. Turn the ganache square over and trim the edges. Cut the ganache into 1-inch squares with a knife dipped in hot water and wiped dry before each cut and wiped clean after each cut.

- If you are dipping squares, temper the chocolate and then dip the squares. Store the dipped chocolates in a cool, dry place, not in the refrigerator.

- If you are making truffles, dust your palms with cocoa powder, roll the ganache squares into balls, and then coat with cocoa powder. Place the truffles in a bowl or plastic bag that contains enough cocoa powder to keep them from sticking together. Store in the refrigerator, but remove them 30 minutes before serving.

✤ Lavender Vanilla Ganache ✤

**About 50 dipped squares
or round truffles**

¾ cup (6 ounces) heavy whipping cream

⅓ cup plus 2 teaspoons (3¾ ounces by weight) invert sugar (stir before measuring)

½ Tahitian vanilla bean, split horizontally

1 tablespoon plus 1 teaspoon dried lavender flowers

10¾ ounces 61% to 70% chocolate, finely chopped

6 tablespoons (3 ounces) unsalted butter with 82% butterfat, very soft (75°F) About ¼ cup melted untempered 41% milk chocolate if dipping squares

Tempered 41% milk chocolate for dipping squares, or unsweetened natural cocoa powder for rolling truffles

The strong floral tones of the lavender stand up to the full-bodied chocolate. If you want to showcase the lavender flavor even more, top each piece of finished chocolate with a lavender flower. Michael makes this ganache with *Lavandula augustifolia* 'Grosso,' a variety that dries without losing its fragrance.

If you are lucky enough to have abundant 'Grosso' lavender plants in your garden, you can harvest the flowers and dry them yourself. Cut the flowers in the early morning, divide them into bunches of no more than 100 stems each, and secure each with a rubber band. Hang them in a dark, well-ventilated place until no moisture remains.

Make the ganache

- Line the bottom and sides of an 8-inch square baking pan with plastic wrap.

- Stir the cream and invert sugar together in a small saucepan. Scrape the vanilla seeds from the bean into the pan and then add the bean. Bring to a boil over medium heat, remove from the heat, and stir in the lavender flowers. Cover the top of the pan with plastic wrap and let steep for 20 minutes.

- While the cream is steeping, put the chocolate in a medium stainless-steel bowl and set the bowl over a pot of simmering water. Heat, stirring occasionally, until the chocolate melts and registers 115°F on an instant-read thermometer. Lift the bowl from the pot.

- Strain the cream through a sieve lined with cheesecloth into a 2-cup liquid measure. When the liquid has run through, pick up the cheesecloth and squeeze the remaining drops into the sieve. If necessary, add cream or discard some of the liquid to bring the volume to 8½ ounces. Check to make sure the temperature is at 115°F and adjust if necessary.

- Pour the chocolate and cream into a 1-quart vessel. Blend with an immersion blender using a stirring motion and making sure to go to the bottom of the vessel. The ganache will thicken, become slightly less shiny, and develop a puddinglike consistency. Add the butter and incorporate it with the immersion blender.

- Pour the ganache into the lined pan. Spread it as evenly as possible with a small offset spatula. Allow the ganache to cool at room temperature until it has set, 2 to 4 hours. Cover the pan with plastic wrap and refrigerate until you are ready to dip squares or roll truffles.

Dip the ganache squares in chocolate or make truffles

- See instructions for tempering chocolate (page 28), dipping chocolates (page 31), and making truffles (page 37).

- Lift the square of ganache from the pan, turn it over onto a work surface, and remove the plastic wrap. If you are dipping squares, apply a thin coat of melted untempered (112°F) 41% milk chocolate to one side of the ganache square with a small offset spatula. (If you are making truffles, don't apply the chocolate coating.) Let the chocolate harden. Turn the ganache square over and trim the edges. Cut the ganache into 1-inch squares with a knife dipped in hot water and wiped dry before each cut and wiped clean after each cut.

- If you are dipping squares, temper the chocolate and then dip the squares. Store the dipped chocolates in a cool, dry place, not in the refrigerator.

- If you are making truffles, dust your palms with cocoa powder, roll the ganache squares into balls, and then coat with cocoa powder. Place the truffles in a bowl or plastic bag that contains enough cocoa powder to keep them from sticking together. Store in the refrigerator, but remove them 30 minutes before serving.

❖ Two-Chocolate Ganache with Cocoa Nib Topping ❖

About 50 dipped squares or round truffles

⅔ cup (5 ounces) heavy whipping cream

⅓ cup (3½ ounces by weight) invert sugar (stir before measuring)

¾ Tahitian vanilla bean, split horizontally

2¾ ounces 41% milk chocolate, finely chopped

6¼ ounces 70% chocolate, finely chopped

7 tablespoons (3½ ounces) unsalted butter with 82% butterfat, very soft (75°F)

About ¼ cup melted untempered 61% to 65% chocolate if dipping squares

Tempered 61% to 65% chocolate if dipping squares

5 tablespoons (1¼ ounces) cocoa nibs, coarsely chopped to half their original size

The infused cream steeps for 24 hours in the refrigerator before you make the ganache, so you need to start this recipe a day in advance. Cocoa nibs, rather than cocoa powder, cover the truffles and are also pressed into the tops of the ganache squares. These small morsels are a new addition to the confectioner's repertoire, and although somewhat astringent, they have a hint of chocolate taste and lend a pleasing crunch to both confections.

Because it is softer than many of the others, this ganache needs an additional day of refrigeration after it is cut into small squares before the squares are dipped or rolled into truffles. The extra time cures the chocolate, enabling it to hold its shape.

Make the ganache

- Stir the cream and invert sugar together in a small saucepan. Scrape the vanilla seeds from the bean into the pan and then add the bean. Bring to a boil over medium heat, remove from the heat, and cover the top of the pan with plastic wrap. When the cream has cooled to room temperature, transfer it to a bowl, cover, and refrigerate overnight.

- Line the bottom and sides of an 8-inch square baking pan with plastic wrap.

- Put both chocolates in a medium stainless-steel bowl and set the bowl over a pot of simmering water. Stir occasionally until the chocolate melts and registers 112°F on an instant-read thermometer. Lift the bowl from the pot.

- When the chocolate is almost at 112°F, remove the cream from the refrigerator. Strain it through a fine-mesh sieve into a small saucepan and heat it to 112°F, stirring occasionally.

- Pour the chocolate and cream into a 1-quart vessel. Blend with an immersion blender using a stirring motion and making sure you reach the bottom of the vessel. The ganache will thicken, become slightly less shiny, and develop a puddinglike consistency. Add the butter and incorporate it with the immersion blender.

- Pour the ganache into the lined pan. Spread it as evenly as possible with a small offset spatula. Allow the ganache to cool at room temperature until it has set, 2 to 4 hours. Cover the pan with plastic wrap and refrigerate until you are ready to dip squares or roll truffles.

Dip the ganache squares in chocolate or make truffles

- See instructions for tempering chocolate (page 28), dipping chocolates (page 31), and making truffles (page 37).

- Lift the square of ganache from the pan, turn it over onto a work surface, and remove the plastic wrap. If you are dipping squares, apply a thin coat of untempered melted (115°F) 61% to 65% chocolate to one side of the ganache square with a small offset spatula. (If you are making truffles, don't apply the chocolate coating.) Let the chocolate harden. Turn the square over and trim the edges. Cut the ganache into 1-inch squares with a knife dipped in hot water and wiped dry before each cut and wiped clean after each cut. Separate the pieces, put them on a sheet pan lined with parchment paper, and cover them with plastic wrap. Refrigerate the squares for 1 day before dipping them in tempered chocolate or rolling them into truffles.

- The next day, remove the squares from the refrigerator. If you are dipping the squares, sprinkle an even layer of the cocoa nibs onto the tops (the sides without the chocolate coating) of the squares. Press the nibs into the squares with a large offset spatula. Temper the chocolate and then dip the squares. Store the dipped chocolates in a cool, dry place, not in the refrigerator.

- If you are making truffles, put the cocoa nibs on a sheet pan. Dust your hands with some of the nibs and roll the ganache squares into balls. Drop the balls onto the sheet pan holding the nibs and shake the pan to cover the balls completely. Leave the truffles on the nib-covered pan (or transfer to a smaller pan if refrigerator space is tight) to keep them from sticking together. Store in the refrigerator, but remove them 30 minutes before serving.

❖ Lemon Verbena Ganache ❖

**About 50 dipped squares
or round truffles**

FOR THE LEMON VERBENA

Several fresh lemon verbena sprigs
(about 100 small leaves)

FOR THE GANACHE

1 cup plus 3 tablespoons (9½
ounces) heavy whipping cream

⅓ cup plus 2 teaspoons (3¾ ounces
by weight) invert sugar (stir before
measuring)

¾ cup dried whole lemon verbena
leaves

9 ounces 61% to 70% chocolate,
finely chopped

5 tablespoons (2½ ounces) unsalted
butter with 82% butterfat, very soft
(75°F)

¼ cup melted untempered 61% to
70% chocolate if dipping squares

Tempered 61% to 70% chocolate
for dipping squares, or unsweetened
natural cocoa powder for rolling
truffles

Lemon verbena is a small shrub with green leaves that possess an intense lemon scent with floral tones. It's so appealing that it is used in perfumes as well as in foods. If you have a plant, or know someone who does, gather the leaves and dry them. If you're not making the ganache right away, gently put the leaves in an airtight container and store at room temperature; they will keep their heady aroma for up to 4 months. Because the lemon verbena needs to be dried and then steeped in cream, you will need to start making the recipe at least 2 days before you plan to make the ganache.

Dry the lemon verbena

- Arrange the lemon verbena sprigs in a single layer on trays of an electric dehydrator or on a baking pan. Set the dehydrator or oven temperature to 105°F, and dry the leaves until no moisture remains and they are brittle, 12 to 24 hours. Carefully separate the leaves from the stems, keeping the leaves whole. You should have ¾ cup leaves. Discard the stems.

Make the ganache

- Stir the cream and invert sugar together in a medium saucepan. Bring to a boil over medium heat, remove from the heat, and stir the lemon verbena leaves into the cream. Cover the top of the pan with plastic wrap. When the cream has cooled to room temperature, transfer it to a bowl, cover, and refrigerate overnight or up to 3 days.

- Line the bottom and sides of an 8-inch square baking pan with plastic wrap.

- Put the chocolate in a medium stainless-steel bowl and set the bowl over a pot of simmering water. Heat, stirring occasionally, until the chocolate melts and registers 115°F on an instant-read thermometer. Lift the bowl from the pot.

- When the chocolate is almost at 115°F, bring the infused cream to a simmer and strain it through a sieve lined with cheesecloth into a 2-cup liquid measure. When the liquid has run through, pick up the cheesecloth and squeeze the remaining drops into the sieve. If necessary, add cream to bring the volume to 9½ ounces. Check to make sure the temperature is at 115°F and adjust if necessary.

- Pour the chocolate and cream into a 1-quart clear vessel. Blend with an immersion blender using a stirring motion and making sure you reach the bottom of the vessel. The ganache will thicken, become slightly less shiny, and develop a puddinglike consistency. Add the butter and incorporate it with the immersion blender.

- Pour the ganache into the lined pan. Spread it as evenly as possible with a small offset spatula. Allow the ganache to cool at room temperature until it has set, 2 to 4 hours. Cover the pan with plastic wrap and refrigerate until you are ready to dip squares or roll truffles.

Dip the ganache squares in chocolate or make truffles

- See instructions for tempering chocolate (page 28), dipping chocolates (page 31), and making truffles (page 37).

- Lift the square of ganache from the pan, turn it over onto a work surface, and remove the plastic wrap. If you are dipping squares, apply a thin coat of melted untempered (115°F) 61% to 70% milk chocolate to one side of the ganache square with a small offset spatula. (If you are making truffles, don't apply the chocolate coating.) Let the chocolate harden. Turn the ganache square over and trim the edges. Cut the ganache into 1-inch squares with a knife dipped in hot water and wiped dry before each cut and wiped clean after each cut.

- If you are dipping squares, temper the chocolate and then dip the squares. Store the dipped chocolates in a cool, dry place, not in the refrigerator.

- If you are making truffles, dust your palms with cocoa powder, roll the ganache squares into balls, and then coat with cocoa powder. Place the truffles in a bowl or plastic bag that contains enough cocoa powder to keep them from sticking together. Store in the refrigerator, but remove them 30 minutes before serving.

❖ Tarragon Ganache with Candied Grapefruit ❖

About 50 dipped squares or round truffles

FOR THE TARRAGON

1 ounce (about 1½ bunches) fresh tarragon sprigs

For the candied grapefruit peel (if dipping squares):

50 strips candied grapefruit peel, each ¾ inch long and ¼ inch wide (see Candied Citrus Peel, page 114)

FOR THE GANACHE

¾ cup plus 2 tablespoons (7 ounces) heavy whipping cream

⅓ cup plus 1 tablespoon (4¼ ounces by weight) invert sugar (stir before measuring)

½ cup dried whole tarragon leaves

9½ ounces 70% chocolate, finely chopped

5 tablespoons (2½ ounces) unsalted butter with 82% butterfat, very soft (75°F)

About ¼ cup melted untempered 61% to 65% chocolate if dipping squares

Tempered 61% to 65% chocolate for dipping squares, or unsweetened natural cocoa powder for truffles

Purchase fresh bunches of tarragon and dry them yourself to make this ganache. The herb will have a fresher, cleaner flavor and will be less expensive than using the small jars sold in the spice sections of grocery stores. Because the tarragon needs to be dried and then steeped overnight in the cream, you need to begin making the recipe at least 2 days before you want to make the ganache.

Each ganache square is topped with a sliver of candied grapefruit before it is dipped. The haunting licorice flavor of the tarragon in the ganache stands up to the citrus tang of the grapefruit, and the chocolate brings both elements together. If you prefer to make truffles instead of dipped squares, omit the grapefruit.

Dry the tarragon

- Arrange the tarragon sprigs in a single layer on trays of an electric dehydrator or on a baking pan. Set the dehydrator or oven temperature to 105°F and dry the tarragon until no moisture remains and the leaves are brittle, 12 to 24 hours. Carefully separate the leaves from the stems, keeping the leaves whole. You should have ½ cup dried leaves. Discard the stems.

Air-dry the candied grapefruit peel

- The grapefruit pieces should air-dry at room temperature overnight before dipping the confections, so a day before you plan to dip the chocolates, remove the 50 strips of peel from the syrup and rinse with cool water to remove the syrup. Arrange the strips on a wire rack placed on a sheet pan. Leave them at room temperature overnight.

Make the ganache

- Stir the cream and invert sugar together in a medium saucepan. Bring to a boil over medium heat, remove from the heat, and stir the tarragon leaves into the cream. Cover the top of the pan with plastic wrap. When it has cooled to room temperature, refrigerate overnight or up to 3 days.

- Line the bottom and sides of an 8-inch square baking pan with plastic wrap.

- Put the chocolate in a medium stainless-steel bowl and set the bowl over a pot of simmering water. Heat, stirring occasionally, until the chocolate melts and registers 115°F on an instant-read thermometer. Lift the bowl from the pot.

- When the chocolate is almost at 115°F, bring the infused cream to a simmer and strain it through a sieve lined with cheesecloth into a 2-cup liquid measure. When the liquid has run through, pick up the cheesecloth and squeeze the remaining drops into the sieve. If necessary, add cream or discard some of the liquid to bring the volume to 8 ½ ounces. Check to make sure the temperature is at 115°F and adjust if necessary.

- Pour the chocolate and cream into a 1-quart clear vessel. Blend with an immersion blender using a stirring motion and making sure you reach the bottom of the vessel. The ganache will thicken, become slightly less shiny, and develop a puddinglike consistency. Add the butter and incorporate it with the immersion blender.

- Pour the ganache into the lined pan. Spread it as evenly as possible with a small offset spatula. Allow the ganache to cool at room temperature until it has set, 2 to 4 hours. Cover it with plastic wrap and refrigerate until you are ready to dip squares or roll truffles.

Dip the ganache squares in chocolate or make truffles

- See instructions for tempering chocolate (page 28), dipping chocolates (page 31), and making truffles (page 37).

- Lift the square of ganache from the pan, turn it over onto a work surface, and remove the plastic wrap. If you are dipping squares, apply a thin coat of melted untempered (115°F) 61% to 65% milk chocolate to one side of the ganache square with a small offset spatula. (If you are making truffles, don't apply the chocolate coating.) Let the chocolate harden. Turn the ganache square over and trim the edges. Cut the ganache into 1-inch squares with a knife dipped in hot water and wiped dry before each cut and wiped clean after each cut.

- If you are dipping squares, press a piece of grapefruit peel diagonally on the top (the side without the chocolate) of each square. Temper the chocolate and then dip the squares. Store the dipped chocolates in a cool, dry place, not in the refrigerator.

- If you are making truffles, dust your palms with cocoa powder, roll the ganache squares into balls, and then coat with cocoa powder. Place the truffles in a bowl or plastic bag that contains enough cocoa powder to keep them from sticking together. Store in the refrigerator, but remove them 30 minutes before serving.

❖ Cardamom Ganache with Cardamom Nougat ❖

About 50 dipped squares or round truffles

FOR THE CARDAMOM NOUGAT (If dipping squares)

¾ cup (6 ounces) granulated cane sugar

¼ cup (1 ounce) cocoa nibs, pulsed briefly 3 times in a coffee grinder reserved for spices to the size of the cardamom seeds

2 teaspoons (¼ ounce) decorticated whole cardamom seeds

FOR THE GANACHE

1 teaspoon decorticated whole cardamom seeds

¾ cup (6 ounces) heavy whipping cream

¼ cup plus 2 teaspoons (3 ounces by weight) invert sugar (stir before measuring)

10½ ounces 61% to 65% chocolate, finely chopped

6 tablespoons (3 ounces) unsalted butter with 82% butterfat, very soft (75°F)

About ¼ cup melted untempered 61% to 65% chocolate if dipping squares

Tempered 61% to 65% chocolate for dipping squares, or unsweetened natural cocoa powder for rolling truffles

Cardamom, the dried fruit of an herb in the ginger family, is the third most expensive spice, after saffron and vanilla. Each fruit, or pod, contains numerous small seeds. Green cardamom, rather than the black or brown, is the type used for confections. Its flavor hints of its ginger heritage, but it is more complex. Whole green pods are available at health-foods stores. If you buy them, break them apart to remove the small seeds. See Resources for where you can purchase decorticated seeds.

You will have nougat left over. Use it to make the ganache again, or sprinkle it over ice cream for a special treat.

Make the cardamom nougat

- Line a sheet pan with parchment paper or a nonstick baking liner, and place next to the stove.

- Put the granulated sugar in a medium heavy-bottomed pot. Use an unlined copper pot if you have one. Place over medium heat and cook, stirring occasionally with a wooden spoon, until the sugar melts. Then continue to cook, without stirring, until the sugar turns dark amber, 4 to 5 minutes. To check the color, dab a small amount of the syrup on a white plate. If any crystals form on the sides of the pan as the sugar darkens, wash them down with a wet pastry brush.

- Remove from the heat and stir in the cocoa nibs and cardamom seeds with the wooden spoon. Pour the nougat onto the prepared sheet pan. Be careful, as it is very hot. Let cool to room temperature. It will become hard and brittle.

- Using your hands, break the nougat into pieces that will comfortably fit in a zippered plastic bag. Slip the pieces into the bag and store at room temperature. The nougat will keep indefinitely stored airtight.

Make the ganache

- Line the bottom and sides of an 8-inch square baking pan with plastic wrap.

- To prepare the cardamom seeds, put them in a plastic bag and crack with a rolling pin to expose the white interiors. Do not crumble them to a powder.

- Stir the cream, invert sugar, and cracked cardamom seeds together in a small saucepan. Bring to a boil over medium heat, remove from the heat, and cover the top of the pan with plastic wrap. Let steep for 15 minutes.

- While the cream is steeping, put the chocolate in a medium stainless-steel bowl and set the bowl over a pot of simmering water. Heat, stirring occasionally, until the chocolate melts and registers 115°F on an instant-read thermometer. Lift the bowl from the pot.

- Strain the cream through a sieve lined with cheesecloth into a 2-cup liquid measure. If necessary, add cream or discard some of the liquid to bring the volume to 7½ ounces. Check to make sure the temperature is at 115°F and adjust if necessary.

- Pour the chocolate and cream into a 1-quart clear vessel. Blend with an immersion blender using a stirring motion and making sure you reach the bottom of the vessel. The ganache will thicken, become slightly less shiny, and develop a puddinglike consistency. Add the butter and incorporate it with the immersion blender.

- Pour the ganache into the lined pan. Spread it as evenly as possible with a small offset spatula. Allow the ganache to cool at room temperature until it has set, 2 to 4 hours. Cover the pan with plastic wrap and refrigerate until you are ready to dip squares or roll truffles.

Assemble the confections

- See instructions for tempering chocolate (page 28), dipping chocolates (page 31), and making truffles (page 37).

- Open a corner of the plastic bag holding the nougat so air can escape, and place the bag on a work surface. Using a rolling pin, break the nougat inside the bag into ⅛-inch pieces by hitting it with the pin. Pour the contents of the bag into a sieve held over a bowl and shake the sieve to release the nougat powder into the bowl. Save the powder that falls through the sieve for another use.

- Lift the square of ganache from the pan, turn it over onto a work surface, and remove the plastic wrap. If you are dipping squares, apply a thin coat of melted untempered (115°F) 61% to 65% chocolate to one side of the ganache square with a small offset spatula. (If you are making truffles, don't apply the chocolate coating.) Let the chocolate harden. Turn the ganache square over and trim the edges. Cut the ganache into 1-inch squares with a knife dipped in hot water and wiped dry before each cut and wiped clean after each cut.

- If you are dipping the squares, sprinkle an even layer of the crumbled nougat onto the tops (the sides without the chocolate coating) of the squares. You will use only about two-thirds of the nougat. Save the remainder for another use. Press the nougat into the squares with a large offset spatula. Temper the chocolate and then dip the squares. Store the dipped chocolates in a cool, dry place, not in the refrigerator.

- If you are making truffles, dust your palms with cocoa powder, roll the ganache squares into balls, and then coat with cocoa powder. Place the truffles in a bowl or plastic bag that contains enough cocoa powder to keep them from sticking together. Store in the refrigerator, but remove them 30 minutes before serving.

OTHER GANACHES AND CENTERS

❖ Varietal Chocolate Ganache ❖

**About 50 dipped squares
or round truffles**

10½ ounces 65% Colombian chocolate, finely chopped

½ cup (4 ounces) heavy whipping cream

⅓ cup plus 2 teaspoons (3¾ ounces by weight) invert sugar (stir before measuring)

5 tablespoons (2½ ounces) unsalted butter with 82% butterfat, very soft (75°F)

About ¼ cup melted untempered 65% Colombian chocolate if dipping squares

Tempered 65% Colombian chocolate for dipping squares, or unsweetened natural cocoa powder for truffles

Many chocolate manufacturers are now highlighting the specific taste profiles of cocoa beans grown in different countries. The Etienne line made by Guittard showcases these different tastes. The Colombian chocolate has a light fruity, spicy taste, while the Ecuadorian chocolate makes a robust ganache with herbal qualities. Cocoa beans from Venezuela produce a deep fruity chocolate with cherry overtones.

This recipe calls for Colombian chocolate, but you can use another 65% varietal instead. Because each chocolate has a unique flavor, the results will be different. To experience the full intensity and specific taste delivered by a varietal chocolate, dip the ganache in the same chocolate you used to make it.

Make the ganache

- Line the bottom and sides of an 8-inch square baking pan with plastic wrap.

- Put the chocolate in a medium stainless-steel bowl and set the bowl over a pot of simmering water. Heat, stirring occasionally, until the chocolate melts and registers 115°F on an instant-read thermometer. Lift the bowl from the pot.

- While the chocolate is melting, stir the cream and invert sugar together in a small saucepan and heat to 115°F.

- Pour the chocolate and cream into a 1-quart clear vessel. Blend with an immersion blender using a stirring motion and making sure you reach the bottom of the vessel. The ganache will thicken, become slightly less shiny, and develop a puddinglike consistency. Add the butter and incorporate it with the immersion blender.

- Pour the ganache into the lined pan. Spread it as evenly as possible with a small offset spatula. Allow the ganache to cool at room temperature until it has set, 2 to 4 hours. Cover the pan with plastic wrap and refrigerate until you are ready to dip squares or roll truffles.

Dip the ganache squares in chocolate or make truffles

- See instructions for tempering chocolate (page 28), dipping chocolates (page 31), and making truffles (page 37).

- Lift the square of ganache from the pan, turn it over onto a work surface, and remove the plastic wrap. If you are dipping squares, apply a thin coat of melted untempered (115°F) 65% Colombian chocolate to one side of the ganache square with a small offset spatula. (If you are making truffles, don't apply the chocolate coating.) Let the chocolate harden. Turn the ganache square over and trim the edges. Cut the ganache into 1-inch squares with a knife dipped in hot water and wiped dry before each cut and wiped clean after each cut.

- If you are dipping squares, temper the chocolate and then dip the squares. Store the dipped chocolates in a cool, dry place, not in the refrigerator.

- If you are making truffles, dust your palms with cocoa powder, roll the ganache squares into balls, and then coat with cocoa powder. Place the truffles in a bowl or plastic bag that contains enough cocoa powder to keep them from sticking together. Store in the refrigerator, but remove them 30 minutes before serving.

❖ Burnt Caramel Base ❖

About 2 cups

3½ cups (1 pound 8½ ounces) granulated cane sugar

1 cup (8 ounces) water

Burnt caramel, Michael's signature flavor, is used as a base for ganache, a drink, and ice cream. Most recipes for caramelizing sugar caution against stirring the sugar once it is melted and cooking it until it is too dark. You can forget about those instructions when making this—the sugar should be burnt. Make the whole recipe and use at your leisure. It will keep refrigerated indefinitely.

- If your kitchen has an exhaust fan, turn it on. Put the sugar in a medium heavy-bottomed pot. Use an unlined copper pot if you have one. Place over medium heat and cook, stirring occasionally with a wooden spoon, until the sugar melts. Then continue to cook, without stirring, until the sugar turns black, about 10 minutes. If any crystals form on the sides of the pan as the sugar darkens, wash them down with a wet pastry brush. Just before it turns black, the sugar syrup may foam up. If it does, reduce the heat to low and, wearing an oven mitt, carefully stir it down. When the sugar syrup is ready, it will smoke and large bubbles will break on the surface.

- While the sugar is cooking, bring the water to a boil in a small saucepan. When the sugar is black, remove the pot from the heat and put a sieve or splatter guard over it. Wearing the oven mitt, slowly pour the hot water into the sugar syrup a little at a time. The mixture will sputter and foam. Be careful, as it is very hot.

- Let the syrup cool to room temperature. Transfer it to a tightly capped storage container and refrigerate until needed.

This photograph illustrates sugar cooked to three stages of caramelization. The darkest shard on the right is the correct hue for Burnt Caramel Base and the Burnt Caramel Sauce. The middle, somewhat lighter piece is the shade for Caramelized Ganache with Sesame Nougat, Fleur de Sel Caramels, Rose Caramel Filling, and Burnt Caramel Pots de Crème. The pale example in the foreground is not cooked enough and won't impart a caramel taste.

❖ Burnt Caramel Ganache ❖

**About 50 dipped squares
or round truffles**

11 ounces 61% to 65% chocolate,
finely chopped

⅔ cup (5 ounces) heavy whipping
cream

¼ cup plus 1 tablespoon (3¼ ounces
by weight) Burnt Caramel Base (page
70)

6 tablespoons (3 ounces) unsalted
butter with 82% butterfat, very soft
(75°F)

About ¼ cup melted untempered
70% chocolate if dipping squares

Tempered 70% chocolate for dipping
squares, or unsweetened natural
cocoa powder for rolling truffles

The burnt caramel adds a complexity that matches the robust tones of the
chocolate. It also plays the same stabilizing role that invert sugar does in other
ganaches. This ganache has an assertive flavor, so it needs an equally assertive chocolate for coating. Use your favorite 70% chocolate.

Because it is softer than many of the others, this ganache needs an
additional day of refrigeration after it is cut into small squares before
the squares are dipped or rolled into truffles. The extra time cures the
chocolate, enabling it to hold its shape.

Make the ganache

- Line the bottom and sides of an 8-inch square baking pan with plastic wrap.

- Put the chocolate in a medium stainless-steel bowl and set the bowl over a pot of simmering water. Heat, stirring occasionally, until the chocolate melts and registers 115°F
  on an instant-read thermometer. Lift the bowl from the pot.

- While the chocolate is melting, stir the cream and caramel base together in a small
  saucepan and heat to 115°F.

- Pour the chocolate and cream into a 1-quart clear vessel. Blend with an immersion
  blender using a stirring motion and making sure you reach the bottom of the vessel. The ganache will thicken, become slightly less shiny, and develop a puddinglike
  consistency. Add the butter and incorporate it with the immersion blender.

- Pour the ganache into the lined pan. Spread it as evenly as possible with a small offset
  spatula. Allow the ganache to cool at room temperature until it has set, 2 to 4 hours.
  Cover the pan with plastic wrap and refrigerate until you are ready to dip squares or
  roll truffles.

Dip the ganache squares in chocolate or make truffles

- See instructions for tempering chocolate (page 28), dipping chocolates (page 31), and
  making truffles (page 37).

- Lift the square of ganache from the pan, turn it over onto a work surface, and remove
  the plastic wrap. If you are dipping squares, apply a thin coat of melted untempered
  (115°F) 70% chocolate to one side of the ganache square with a small offset spatula.
  (If you are making truffles, don't apply the chocolate coating.) Let the chocolate
  harden. Turn the ganache square over and trim the edges. Cut the ganache into
  1-inch squares with a knife dipped in hot water and wiped dry before each cut and

wiped clean after each cut. Separate the pieces, put them on a sheet pan lined with parchment paper, and cover them with plastic wrap. Refrigerate the squares for 1 day before dipping them in tempered chocolate or rolling them into truffles.

- The next day, remove the squares from the refrigerator. If you are dipping squares, temper the chocolate and then dip the squares. Store the dipped chocolates in a cool, dry place, not in the refrigerator.

- If you are making truffles, dust your palms with cocoa powder, roll the ganache squares into balls, and then coat with cocoa powder. Place the truffles in a bowl or plastic bag that contains enough cocoa powder to keep them from sticking together. Store in the refrigerator, but remove them 30 minutes before serving.

About 50 pieces

FOR THE SESAME NOUGAT

½ cup plus 1 tablespoon (4 ounces) granulated cane sugar

⅓ cup (1¼ ounces) sesame seeds, preferably natural unhulled

FOR THE GANACHE

⅓ cup (2½ ounces) granulated cane sugar

⅔ cup (5 ounces) heavy whipping cream

11¼ ounces 41% milk chocolate, finely chopped

2 ounces 70% chocolate, finely chopped

About ¼ cup melted untempered 61% to 65% chocolate for coating ganache squares

Tempered 61% to 65% chocolate for finishing the chocolates

The day we tested this recipe in the Recchiuti Confections kitchen, one of the confectioners was making a large batch of it for shipment to customers. She scooped the finished ganache into a plastic trough designed to slide along a plastic rectangle with nickel-sized cutouts. As she carefully slid the trough, ganache was deposited into the cutouts. Another worker rapped a round cutter on a paper-thin sheet of sesame nougat to make wafers. After the ganache set, each piece was pressed onto a nougat disk and then taken to the enrober to be bathed in chocolate. This is a less complicated version, but just as delicious.

Make the sesame nougat

- Line a sheet pan with parchment paper or a nonstick baking liner, and place next to the stove.

- Put the sugar in a medium heavy-bottomed pot. Use an unlined copper pot if you have one. Place over medium heat and cook, stirring occasionally with a wooden spoon, until the sugar melts. Then continue to cook, without stirring, until the sugar turns dark amber, 4 to 5 minutes. To check the color, dab a small amount of the syrup on a white plate. If any crystals form on the sides of the pan as the sugar darkens, wash them down with a wet pastry brush.

- Remove from the heat and stir in the sesame seeds with the wooden spoon. Pour the nougat onto the prepared pan. Be careful, as it is very hot. Let cool to room temperature. It will become hard and brittle.

- Using your hands, break the nougat into pieces that will comfortably fit in a zippered plastic bag. Slip the pieces into the bag and store at room temperature. The nougat will keep indefinitely stored airtight.

Make the ganache

- Line the bottom and sides of an 8-inch square baking pan with plastic wrap.

- Put the sugar in a medium heavy-bottomed pot. Use an unlined copper pot if you have one. Place over medium heat and cook, stirring occasionally with a wooden spoon, until the sugar melts. Then continue to cook, without stirring, until the sugar turns dark amber, 4 to 5 minutes. To check the color, dab a small amount of the syrup on a white plate. If any crystals form on the sides of the pan as the sugar darkens, wash them down with a wet pastry brush.

- While the sugar is cooking, bring the cream to a boil in a small saucepan over medium heat. When the sugar is the correct shade, remove the pot from the heat and put a sieve or splatter guard over it. Wearing an oven mitt, slowly pour the hot cream into the sugar syrup a little at a time. The mixture will sputter and foam. Be careful, as it is very hot. Let the caramel cool to 112°F. This will take about 10 minutes.

- While the caramel is cooling, put both chocolates in a medium stainless-steel bowl and set the bowl over a pot of simmering water. Heat, stirring occasionally, until the chocolate melts and registers 112°F on an instant-read thermometer. Lift the bowl from the pot.

- Pour the chocolate and caramel into a 1-quart vessel. Blend with an immersion blender using a stirring motion and making sure you reach the bottom of the vessel. The ganache will thicken, look like glossy clay, and have the consistency of very loose taffy.

- Pour the ganache into the lined pan. Spread it as evenly as possible with a small offset spatula. Allow the ganache to cool at room temperature until it has set, 2 to 4 hours. Cover the pan with plastic wrap and refrigerate until you are ready to finish the confections.

Assemble the confections

- See instructions for tempering chocolate (page 28) and dipping chocolates (page 31).

- Open a corner of the plastic bag holding the nougat so air can escape, and place the bag on a work surface. Using a rolling pin, break the nougat inside the bag into ⅛-inch pieces by hitting it with the pin. Pour the contents of the bag into a sieve held over a bowl and shake the sieve to release the nougat powder into the bowl. Save the powder that falls through the sieve for another use.

- You can make square or round chocolates for dipping. Lift the square of ganache from the pan, turn it over onto a work surface, and remove the plastic wrap. If you are dipping squares, apply a thin coat of melted untempered (115°F) 61% to 65% chocolate to one side of the ganache square with a small offset spatula. (If you are making balls, don't apply the chocolate coating.) Let the chocolate harden. Turn the ganache square over and trim the edges. Cut the ganache into 1-inch squares with a knife dipped in hot water and wiped dry before each cut and wiped clean after each cut.

- If you are dipping squares, sprinkle an even layer of the crumbled nougat onto the tops (the sides without the chocolate coating) of the squares. Press the nougat into the squares with a large offset spatula. Temper the chocolate, and then dip the squares in the chocolate.

- If you are making balls, spread the nougat on a sheet pan. Dust your hands with some of the nougat and roll the ganache squares into balls. Drop the balls into the baking pan holding the nougat and shake the pan to cover the balls completely. Temper the chocolate, and then dip the balls in the chocolate.

- Store the dipped chocolates in a cool, dry place, not in the refrigerator.

About 50 pieces

FOR THE HONEYCOMB BRITTLE

¼ cup (2 ounces) water

1½ cups (10½ ounces) granulated cane sugar

¼ cup (2⅔ ounces by weight) light corn syrup

1 tablespoon baking soda

FOR THE GANACHE

12¾ ounces white chocolate, finely chopped

¾ cup (6 ounces) heavy whipping cream

2 tablespoons (1¼ ounces by weight) unhopped barley-malt syrup

3 tablespoons (1½ ounces) unsalted butter with 82% butterfat, very soft (75°F)

About ¼ cup melted untempered 41% milk chocolate for coating ganache squares

Tempered 41% milk chocolate for finishing the chocolates

This confection gets its name from its covering of golden brittle, which in cross-section is reminiscent of a honeycomb. The ganache is shaped into balls, which are then sheathed in chunks of the brittle and dipped in chocolate, resulting in a rustic-looking confection.

You can use a whisk, rather than an immersion blender, to make this ganache. The high dose of cocoa butter in the white chocolate helps the ganache emulsify more readily than others. The ganache must sit overnight (or up to 3 days) before shaping into rounds.

Make the honeycomb brittle

- Line a sheet pan with parchment paper or a nonstick baking liner and place next to the stove.

- Put the water, sugar, and corn syrup in a heavy-bottomed pot, preferably narrow and at least 6 inches deep. Stir with a wooden spoon to mix the water into the sugar and corn syrup. Place over medium heat and cook, stirring occasionally, until the sugar melts. Then continue to cook, without stirring, until the syrup registers 300°F on a candy thermometer, 8 to 10 minutes. If any crystals form on the sides of the pan as the mixture darkens, wash them down with a wet pastry brush.

- Remove from the heat, add the baking soda, and whisk 3 or 4 times. The brittle will climb to the top of the pot and turn golden brown. Pour it onto the prepared pan before it overflows. Don't scrape the pot and don't spread the brittle. It will stay puffed up and look like molten lava. Let cool to room temperature. It will become hard and brittle.

- Using your hands, break the brittle into pieces that will comfortably fit in a zippered plastic bag. Slip the pieces into the bag and store at room temperature. The brittle will keep indefinitely stored airtight.

Make the ganache

- Line the bottom and sides of an 8-inch square baking pan with plastic wrap.

- Put the chocolate in a medium stainless-steel bowl and set the bowl over a pot of simmering water. Heat, stirring occasionally, until the chocolate melts and registers 112°F on an instant-read thermometer. Lift the bowl from the pot.

- While the chocolate is melting, bring the cream to a simmer in a medium saucepan over medium heat. Remove from the heat and stir in the malt syrup. Check to make sure the temperature is at 112°F and adjust if necessary.

- Pour the hot cream into the chocolate and whisk by hand until well blended. Whisk in the butter. The ganache will not undergo the dramatic change that occurs when making ganache with darker chocolate. It will remain more liquid.

- Pour the ganache into the lined pan. Spread it as evenly as possible with a small offset spatula. Allow the ganache to cool at room temperature until it has set, 2 to 4 hours. Cover the pan with plastic wrap. Let it sit at room temperature for at least overnight. If you have time, allow to sit for up 3 days. It will be stiffer and easier to roll.

Assemble the confections

- See instructions for tempering chocolate (page 28) and dipping chocolates (page 31). Line 2 sheet pans with parchment paper.

- Open a corner of the plastic bag holding the nougat so air can escape, and place the bag on a work surface. Using a rolling pin, break the brittle inside the bag into ⅛-inch pieces by hitting it with the pin. Pour the contents of the bag into a sieve held over a bowl and shake the sieve to release the brittle powder into the bowl. Save the powder that falls through the sieve for another use. Spread the brittle on one of the prepared pans.

- Lift the square of ganache from the pan, turn it over onto a work surface, and remove the plastic wrap. Cut the ganache into 1-inch squares with a knife dipped in hot water and wiped dry before each cut and wiped clean after each cut.

- Dust your hands with some of the brittle and roll the ganache squares into balls. Drop the balls onto the pan holding the brittle and shake the pan to cover the balls completely. Temper the chocolate, and then dip the brittle-coated balls in the chocolate. As the confections are dipped, put them on the second prepared pan.

- Store the dipped chocolates in a cool, dry place, not in the refrigerator.

❖ Fleur de Sel Caramels ❖

About 50 pieces

Flavorless vegetable oil for the pan

1½ cups (10½ ounces) granulated cane sugar

½ Tahitian vanilla bean, split horizontally

1 cup (8 ounces) heavy whipping cream

2 tablespoons (1⅓ ounces by weight) light corn syrup

1 tablespoon (½ ounce) unsalted butter with 82% butterfat, chilled

½ teaspoon *fleur de sel* in fine grains

Tempered 61% to 70% chocolate if dipping

Fleur de sel in fine grains for finishing confections

Fleur de sel, the mineral-rich and intensely flavored crystals that form on the surface of shallow beds filled with seawater, has made a comeback in recent years. Although this prized salt has been harvested by hand for centuries along Europe's west coast, the growth in industrial salt production after World War II pushed it into the background. Nowadays, chefs, recognizing the superior character of the salt, sprinkle a little on a finished dish to add a burst of flavor.

Salt has always been a subtle, but important, ingredient for caramels, balancing their sweetness. Michael stirs *fleur de sel* into the caramel just before it comes off the stove. The crystals add both flavor and crunch to the finished confections.

Unlike many other caramel recipes, Michael adds the corn syrup after the sugar colors. He has discovered that mixing it in at the beginning of cooking inhibits caramelization. These caramels are also delicious without the chocolate coating; simply cut into sticks and wrap individually.

Make the caramels

- Line the bottom of an 8-inch square baking pan with parchment paper. Lightly coat the paper and the sides of the pan with flavorless vegetable oil.

- Put the sugar in a medium heavy-bottomed pot. Use an unlined copper pot if you have one. Scrape the seeds from the vanilla bean into the pot. Place over medium heat and cook, stirring occasionally with a wooden spoon, until the sugar melts. Then continue to cook, without stirring, until the sugar turns dark amber, 5 to 6 minutes. To check the color, dab a small amount of the syrup on a white plate. If any crystals form on the sides of the pan as the sugar darkens, wash them down with a wet pastry brush.

- While the sugar is cooking, bring the cream to a boil in a small saucepan over medium heat. When the sugar is the correct shade, stir in the corn syrup. Remove the pot from the heat and put a sieve or splatter guard over it. Wearing an oven mitt, slowly pour the hot cream into the sugar syrup a little at a time. The mixture will sputter and foam. Be careful, as it is very hot.

- When the bubbling subsides, return the pan to medium heat and cook undisturbed until the mixture registers 252°F on a candy thermometer, about 5 minutes. Remove from the heat, immediately add the butter, and stir with the wooden spoon. Add the salt and stir until evenly distributed.

- Pour the caramel into the prepared pan and let cool at room temperature.

Assemble the caramels

- If you are dipping the caramels in chocolate, see instructions for tempering chocolate (page 28) and dipping chocolates (page 31).

- Invert the pan of cooled caramel onto a work surface. Peel off the parchment paper.

- If you are not dipping the caramels, using a ruler as a guide, cut the caramel square into sticks 3 inches long and 1 inch wide with a lightly oiled knife. Enclose each stick in transparent wrap. Store in a cool place, not in the refrigerator.

- If you are dipping the caramels in chocolate, line a sheet pan with parchment paper. Using a ruler as a guide, cut the caramel square into 1-inch squares with a lightly oiled knife. Temper the 61% to 70% chocolate and then dip the squares. Place them on the prepared pan. Sprinkle each square with a few grains of fleur de sel before the chocolate sets.

- When the chocolate has set, store the caramels in a cool, dry place, not in the refrigerator.

Molded Chocolates

The fillings for molded chocolates are softer and less viscous than those used for dipping, characteristics that help them flow readily into molds but make them too soft for shaping truffles. They should be at room temperature to flow properly, so make these fillings the same day that you line the molds with chocolate. Don't be tempted to make them ahead and refrigerate them until needed. Reheating them can cause them to separate and look curdled.

An inexpensive plastic squirt bottle is the best tool for filling the indentations of the chocolate-lined molds. It prevents drips and lets you put the filling precisely where it should go.

Three of these fillings—the ginger, star anise–pink peppercorn, and Kona coffee ganaches—rely on infusions for their flavor. The star anise–pink peppercorn infusion needs an additional straining to prevent a gritty ganache. A sieve lined with cheesecloth will capture most of the grounds, but a second pass through a gold coffee filter eliminates all of them.

The Rose Caramel Filling (page 82) also needs special attention. Because the filling is a liquid caramel, not a chewy one, it needs to set overnight in the lined molds at room temperature to develop a thin skin before the bottoms of the molds are covered with chocolate.

Nut lovers will want to try the Chocolate and Nut Butter Filling (page 89). It is easy to make and a few pieces of the finished confections will satisfy the most intense nut craving.

About 50 pieces, depending on the capacity of the molds

1¼ cups (9 ounces) granulated cane sugar

¾ cup (6 ounces) heavy whipping cream

3 tablespoons (2 ounces by weight) invert sugar (stir before measuring)

6 tablespoons (3 ounces) unsalted butter with 82% butterfat, chilled

1 drop rose geranium oil

Tempered white chocolate for lining the molds

Tempered 61% to 65% chocolate for covering the bottoms of the molds

Confectioners in the Recchiuti Confections kitchen pipe thin stripes of dark chocolate into the indentations of narrow molds and then line them with the chocolate before filling them with this intensely fragrant caramel. The heady aroma comes from oil of rose geranium (see Resources). Only a single drop of the oil is added—you need an eye dropper to measure it—to flavor the whole batch. Because the flavor is so strong, you need to use small molds for these confections.

The filling is a liquid caramel, not a chewy one, so it needs to set overnight in the lined molds at room temperature to develop a thin skin before the bottom of the mold is covered with chocolate. This means that you will have to temper chocolate twice to make these candies—once to line the molds and again the next day to cover the bottoms. The glory of these confections is worth this minor inconvenience.

Make the filling

- Put the sugar in a medium heavy-bottomed pot. Use an unlined copper pot if you have one. Place over medium heat and cook, stirring occasionally with a wooden spoon, until the sugar melts. Then continue to cook, without stirring, until the sugar turns dark amber, 5 to 6 minutes. To check the color, dab a small amount of the syrup on a white plate. If any crystals form on the sides of the pan as the sugar darkens, wash them down with a wet pastry brush.

- While the sugar is cooking, stir the cream and invert sugar together in a medium saucepan and bring to a boil over medium heat. When the sugar is the correct shade, remove the pot from the heat and put a sieve or splatter guard over it. Wearing an oven mitt, slowly pour the hot cream mixture into the sugar syrup a little at a time. The mixture will sputter and foam. Be careful, as it is very hot.

- Return the pot to low heat and cook, scraping the bottom with the wooden spoon to incorporate any caramel stuck to the bottom. Stir in the butter.

- Strain the caramel through a fine-mesh sieve into a bowl. When it has cooled to 85°F, using an eye dropper, add the rose oil and then stir to distribute evenly.

Temper the chocolate, line the molds, and finish the confections

- See instructions for tempering chocolate (page 28) and molding chocolates (page 39). Line the indentations in the molds with tempered white chocolate.

- Pour the caramel into a plastic squirt bottle and fill the indentations to within ⅛ inch of the top of the molds. Tap the filled molds on a work surface to even out the filling. Let the molds sit overnight at 65° to 70°F until the filling has fully set.

- The next day, temper a small amount of 61% to 65% chocolate and cover the bottoms of the molds. (Or, temper a larger amount and use what is left over to make a bark.) Let sit for at least 1 hour at room temperature to set the chocolate fully. When the chocolate has set, rap the molds on a work surface to release the individual chocolates, or leave the finished chocolates in the molds and release them just before serving.

- Store the finished chocolates in a cool, dry place, not in the refrigerator.

❖ Kona Coffee Ganache ❖

About 50 pieces, depending on the capacity of the molds

¼ cup (½ ounce) dark-roast whole Kona coffee beans

¾ cup plus 2 tablespoons (7 ounces) heavy whipping cream

4½ ounces 41% milk chocolate

5 ounces 62% to 65% chocolate, finely chopped

½ cup plus 1 tablespoon (6 ounces by weight) invert sugar (stir before measuring)

1 teaspoon brandy

Tempered 65% chocolate for lining the molds and covering the bottoms of the molds

Kona coffee beans, grown in Hawaii, are low in acid and have a mild, mellow taste that doesn't compete with the chocolate in this ganache, but instead adds complexity. You can use another type of coffee bean, but be sure it does not have an aggressive flavor.

This is the only ganache recipe in the book that infuses the cream without the invert sugar. Michael learned this adaptation after trial and error. The coffee beans weren't imparting their full goodness to the cream, so, as an experiment, he tried adding the invert sugar after the cream steeped. That solved the problem. He can only speculate that the sugar somehow seals the beans, inhibiting the release of their flavor.

Choose chocolate that is floral and not too tannic, such as Scharffen Berger 62% or Guittard L'Harmonie.

Make the ganache

- Break the coffee beans into pieces about one-fourth their original size. You can do this either in a coffee grinder or by placing them between sheets of parchment paper and hitting them with a rolling pin.

- Bring the cream to a boil in a small saucepan over medium heat. Remove from the heat and stir the coffee beans into the cream. Cover the top of the pan with plastic wrap and let steep for 30 minutes.

- While the cream is steeping, put both chocolates in a medium stainless-steel bowl and set the bowl over a pot of simmering water. Stir occasionally until the chocolate melts and registers 112°F on an instant-read thermometer. Lift the bowl from the pot.

- Strain the cream through a sieve lined with cheesecloth into a 2-cup liquid measure. Stir the invert sugar into the cream. If necessary, add cream or discard some of the liquid to bring the volume to 11 ounces. Check to make sure the temperature is at 112°F and adjust if necessary.

- Pour the chocolate and cream into a 1-quart vessel. Blend with an immersion blender using a stirring motion and making sure you reach the bottom of the vessel.

The ganache will thicken, become slightly less shiny, and develop a puddinglike consistency. Add the brandy and incorporate it with the immersion blender. Let the ganache cool to 85°F.

Temper the chocolate, line the molds, and finish the confections

- See instructions for tempering chocolate (page 28) and molding chocolates (page 39). Line the indentations in the molds with tempered chocolate.

- Pour the ganache into a plastic squirt bottle and fill the indentations to within ⅛ inch of the top of the molds. Tap the filled molds on a work surface to even out the ganache. Refrigerate the molds until the filling has just set, about 20 minutes. Don't overchill, or the chocolate will go out of temper when you cover the filling.

- Cover the bottoms of the molds with tempered chocolate and let sit for at least 1 hour at room temperature to set the chocolate fully. When the chocolate has set, rap the molds on a work surface to release the individual chocolates, or leave the finished chocolates in the molds and release them just before serving.

- Store the finished chocolates in a cool, dry place, not in the refrigerator.

❖ Ginger Ganache ❖

About 50 pieces, depending on the capacity of the molds

3 quarter-sized slices (½ ounce) crystallized ginger

⅔ cup (5 ounces) heavy whipping cream

¼ cup plus 3 tablespoons (4½ ounces by weight) invert sugar (stir before measuring)

1½ ounces peeled fresh ginger, roughly chopped

7 ounces 61% to 70% chocolate, finely chopped

Tempered white chocolate for lining the molds and finishing the chocolates

At Recchiuti Confections, the confectioners apply flecks of gold leaf to the indentations of heart-shaped molds before lining them with chocolate, and then drop bits of crystallized ginger into the lined molds before filling them with this ganache. Different-shaped molds would work equally well. If you prefer dark chocolate, line the indentations in the molds with the same chocolate you used for the ganache, instead of white chocolate.

Use Australian crystallized ginger. It has a subtle texture that is not in jarring contrast to the ganache. Other gingers are sometimes hard and leathery. Be sure to cut and rinse the ginger several hours in advance of when you need it, so it will have time to dry fully.

Make the ganache

- Cut the crystallized ginger into ⅛-inch dice. Rinse off the sugar crystals with cool water and pat the ginger with a kitchen towel. Arrange the pieces on a baking rack and let the pieces dry completely at room temperature for several hours.

- Stir the cream and invert sugar together in a medium saucepan. Bring to a boil over medium heat, remove from the heat, and stir the fresh ginger into the cream. Cover the top of the pan with plastic wrap and let steep for 25 minutes.

- While the cream is steeping, put the chocolate in a medium stainless-steel bowl and set the bowl over a pot of simmering water. Heat, stirring occasionally, until the chocolate melts and registers 115°F on an instant-read thermometer. Lift the bowl from the pot.

- Strain the cream through a fine-mesh sieve into a 2-cup liquid measure. If necessary, add cream or discard some of the liquid to bring the volume to 8½ ounces. Check to make sure the temperature is at 115°F and adjust if necessary.

- Pour the chocolate and cream into a 1-quart vessel. Blend with an immersion blender using a stirring motion and making sure you reach the bottom of the vessel. The ganache will thicken, become slightly less shiny, and develop a puddinglike consistency. Let the ganache cool to 85°F.

Temper the chocolate, line the molds, and finish the confections

- See instructions for tempering chocolate (page 28) and molding chocolates (page 39). Line the indentations in the molds with tempered white chocolate. When the chocolate has set, after about 30 minutes, put a few pieces of crystallized ginger into each indentation.

- Pour the ganache into a plastic squirt bottle and fill the indentations to within ⅛ inch of the top of the molds. Tap the filled molds on a work surface to even out the ganache. Refrigerate the molds until the filling has just set, about 20 minutes. Don't overchill, or the chocolate will go out of temper when you cover the filling.

- Cover the bottoms of the molds with tempered white chocolate and let sit for at least 1 hour at room temperature to set the chocolate fully. When the chocolate has set, rap the molds on a work surface to release the individual chocolates, or leave the finished chocolates in the molds and release them just before serving.

- Store the finished chocolates in a cool, dry place, not in the refrigerator.

❖ STAR ANISE–PINK PEPPERCORN GANACHE ❖

A pair of chocolates complements the assertive flavors in this ganache. The milk chocolate softens the spices and the dark chocolate tames the sweetness. The star anise pod, harvested from *Illicium verum*, a tree in the Magnolia family, contains a small brown seed with a spicy licorice flavor in each of its eight points. Pink peppercorns are entirely different from the berries that are processed into green, white, and black pepper. They grow on trees instead of vines and have an assertive floral, spicy taste with a hint of pine.

Grind the spices in an inexpensive coffee grinder reserved for spices. They should be finely ground, but not to a powder. A single pass through a cheese-cloth-lined sieve won't capture all the fine bits of spice, so you must strain the cream twice, once through cheesecloth and once through a gold coffee filter, to avoid a gritty ganache. The cream drips slowly through the coffee filter, so be patient. Stir the contents and tap the side of the filter to keep it flowing.

continued next page . . .

Star Anise–Pink Peppercorn Ganache (continued)

About 50 pieces, depending on the capacity of the molds

5½ ounces 41% milk chocolate, finely chopped

4½ ounces 70% chocolate, finely chopped

1⅛ cups (9 ounces) heavy whipping cream

½ cup plus 2 tablespoons (6½ ounces by weight) invert sugar (stir before measuring)

3 tablespoons (½ ounce) finely ground star anise

1 tablespoon (¼ ounce) finely ground pink peppercorns

Tempered 41% milk chocolate for lining the molds and finishing the chocolates

Make the ganache

- Put both chocolates in a medium stainless-steel bowl and set the bowl over a pot of simmering water. Stir occasionally until the chocolate melts and registers 112°F on an instant-read thermometer. Lift the bowl from the pot.

- While the chocolate is melting, stir the cream and invert sugar together in a medium saucepan. Bring to a boil over medium heat, remove from the heat, and stir the spices into the cream. Cover the top of the pan with plastic wrap and let steep for 5 to 8 minutes.

- Strain the cream through a sieve lined with cheesecloth into a bowl. When the liquid has run through, pick up the cheesecloth and squeeze the remaining drops into the sieve. Strain the liquid again through a gold coffee filter into a 2-cup liquid measure. If necessary, add cream or discard some of the liquid to bring the volume to 11¾ ounces. Check to make sure the temperature is at 112°F and adjust if necessary.

- Pour the chocolate and cream into a 1-quart clear vessel. Blend the mixture with an immersion blender using a stirring motion and making sure you reach the bottom of the vessel. The ganache will thicken, become slightly less shiny, and develop a puddinglike consistency. Let the ganache cool to 85°F.

Temper the chocolate, line the molds, and finish the confections

- See instructions for tempering chocolate (page 28) and molding chocolates (page 39). Line the indentations in the molds with tempered milk chocolate.

- Pour the ganache into a plastic squirt bottle and fill the indentations to within ⅛ inch of the top of the molds. Tap the filled molds on a work surface to even out the ganache. Refrigerate the molds until the filling has just set, about 20 minutes. Don't overchill, or the chocolate will go out of temper when you cover the filling.

- Cover the bottoms of the molds with tempered 41% milk chocolate and let sit for at least 1 hour at room temperature to set the chocolate fully. When the chocolate has set, rap the molds on a work surface to release the individual chocolates, or leave the finished chocolates in the molds and release them just before serving.

- Store the finished chocolates in a cool, dry place, not in the refrigerator.

❖ Chocolate and Nut Butter Filling ❖

Europeans make some of the best nut pastes in the world by caramelizing the nuts and then putting them through machines that crush and roll them into silken masses. Michael had coveted these machines for years. By extraordinary coincidence, the day we tested this recipe, a friend called Michael from Germany. He was at an auction of baking and confectionery equipment, and a few nut-paste-making machines were on the block. Did Michael want one? You know the answer.

The flavor of this filling is not as intense as the fillings made from European pastes, but it does have a clean taste of the nut. Buy a smooth nut butter made from roasted nuts and without added salt or sugar. Because this filling is soft, it is best to use it only for molded chocolates.

About 50 pieces, depending on the capacity of the molds

50 medium-sized whole hazelnuts

9 ounces 41% milk chocolate, finely chopped

Scant ¾ cup (5⅔ ounces by weight) smooth hazelnut butter, at room temperature

Tempered 41% milk chocolate for lining the molds and finishing the chocolates

Roast and skin the hazelnuts

- Preheat the oven to 350°F. Line the bottom of a sheet pan with parchment paper.

- Spread the hazelnuts on the prepared pan in a single layer. Roast the nuts until the skins start to darken and shrivel, about 8 minutes.

- Remove the nuts from the oven. As soon as they are cool enough to handle, rub them in batches in a kitchen towel to remove the skins. Not every bit will come off.

Make the filling

- Put the chocolate in a medium stainless-steel bowl and set the bowl over a pot of simmering water. Stir occasionally until the chocolate melts and registers 112°F on an instant-read thermometer. Lift the bowl from the pot.

- While the chocolate is melting, stir the hazelnut butter with a rubber spatula to distribute any oil that may have separated. When the chocolate is ready, mix the hazelnut butter into the chocolate with the spatula. Check the temperature; it should not exceed 85°F. Let the filling cool if it is too hot.

continued next page . . .

CHOCOLATE AND NUT BUTTER FILLING (CONTINUED)

Temper the chocolate, line the molds, and finish the confections

- See instructions for tempering chocolate (page 28) and molding chocolates (page 39).

- Line the indentations in the molds with tempered 41% milk chocolate.

- After the chocolate has set, drop a hazelnut into each indentation. The tops of the nuts must be at least 1/8 inch below the top of the indentations. If any of the nuts are too tall, cut them in half.

- Pour the filling into a plastic squirt bottle and fill the indentations to within 1/8 inch of the top of the molds. Tap the filled molds on a work surface to even out the filling. Refrigerate the molds until the filling has just set, about 20 minutes. Don't overchill, or the chocolate will go out of temper when you cover the filling.

- Cover the bottoms of the molds with tempered 41% milk chocolate and let sit for at least 1 hour at room temperature to set the chocolate fully. When the chocolate has set, rap the molds on a work surface to release the individual chocolates, or leave the finished chocolates in the molds and release them just before serving.

- Store the finished chocolates in a cool, dry place, not in the refrigerator.

Variations

- Use blanched almonds and smooth almond butter, made from roasted nuts and without added salt or sugar, in place of the hazelnuts and hazelnut butter.

- For a more rustic confection, mold the filling in chocolate-lined paper liners for muffin cups. See Peanut Butter Pucks (page 116) for directions on lining the paper liners.

Michael at the Farmers' Market

In 1993, a farmers' market made its debut on Saturday mornings in a parking lot directly facing the front of San Francisco's Ferry Building, on the waterfront at the foot of Market Street. The stately building, with its tall clock tower, lent a sense of urban history to the bustling scene. But there was a new future for the structure. Over the years, it had been divided into nondescript office spaces that hid its stature and fine architectural lines. Plans were afoot to restore it to its former grandeur and to include a permanent market-place on its ample ground floor.

When the restoration work got underway, the farmers' market was moved a few blocks north to another parking lot. Each Saturday, the farmers and other vendors unfurled umbrellas and assembled pop-ups, and then sold their wares, everything from organic tomatoes, melons, squashes, greens of every description, potatoes, and other seasonal crops to baked goods, olive oils, nuts, and even espresso to fuel the shoppers. One thing was missing, though: no one sold chocolates.

Although Recchiuti Confections was a whole-sale operation without a retail venue at the time, locals were becoming aware of these new chocolates. When Chuck Williams, founder of Williams-Sonoma, was given a box for his birthday, he was so impressed that he introduced Sibella Kraus, then the director of the farmers' market, to the confections. She in turn contacted Michael and asked him to submit chocolates to the farmers' market board for a tasting. The board immediately invited Michael to be a part-time vendor for the summer. Michael saw it as a promotional opportunity; he didn't think he would actually sell much chocolate. At his first market appearance, everything disappeared in one hour and his expectations changed. Each week he brought more chocolates. Soon the board invited him to become a permanent member of the market.

Most of the vendors had white umbrellas or pop-ups. To make his space distinctive, Michael bought a red pop-up. It was easy to spot in the crowd, but after a few hot days, Michael realized most people had chosen white because it reflected, rather than absorbed, the sun's rays.

The market provided an outlet for Michael's creative imagination. In addition to the more formal boxes of chocolates, he started bringing items that eventually evolved into his snack line, which includes marshmallows, s'more kits, brownies, peanut butter pucks, sesame tuiles, and chocolate-covered caramelized nuts. It wasn't possible

to distribute ice cream to a wholesale market, but packing pints and taking them to the market was easy and let him experiment. The market itself provided inspiration. Perfect berries and Meyer lemons went back to the Recchiuti Confections kitchen and were swirled with cream and eggs in the ice-cream maker.

During the rainy winters and on foggy summer days, Michael bundled up in colorful scarfs and a hat chosen from his ample supply. Sometimes he wore a bright orange knit cap pulled down over his ears, other times a wool cap with a brim. With his beard, and dressed in cargo pants and Italian shoes, he looked more like a member of a rock band than a chocolate maker.

There was always a crowd in front of his table. People jostled to get within reach of the samples. There were loyal regulars who returned every week to sate their chocolate craving and offer their opinions of new creations—too much lavender in the ganache, not enough sugar in an ice cream, or "that brownie is perfect, don't touch it."

In March 2003, the farmers' market moved back to the front of the Ferry Building, not to the parking lot this time, but to the sidewalk directly in front of the building and to space along the piers behind it. Recchiuti Confections had leased a permanent spot inside the structure, but because it wasn't ready, Michael continued to sell chocolates outdoors alongside farmers selling produce.

Finally the retail spot was finished and Recchiuti Confections opened in July 2003. The sleek, sophisticated alcove, with custom-made display cases and one-of-a-kind dishes to hold the chocolates, is a far cry from the wind-blown red pop-up in the parking lot. But the popular snacks add an air of whimsy to the space.

SNACKS

When Michael started making marshmallows and s'more kits in addition to his ganache-filled signature chocolates, he dubbed them snacks because they were a less formal addition to his repertoire. As the business grew, he thought of other fanciful treats that also fit into the snack category: Key lime pears, sesame tuiles, peanut butter pucks, brownies, whoopie pies, and chocolate-covered caramelized nuts.

This chapter is a selection of these delightful creations as well as recipes for cookies, cupcakes, and ice-cream sandwiches. Many can be prepared quickly without a mixer. We have also included Double–Dark Chocolate Soufflés (page 128) and Burnt Caramel Pots de Crème (page 126), which are a bit more elegant than snacks and will fill the bill when you need a grand finale for a dinner party.

30 crackers

⅓ cup (3 ounces) whole milk

1 tablespoon plus 1 teaspoon pure vanilla extract, preferably Madagascar Bourbon

4 tablespoons (2 ounces by weight) mild-flavored honey such as clover or orange blossom

1 cup (5 ounces) unbleached all-purpose flour

1 cup plus 3 tablespoons (5¼ ounces) whole-wheat flour, preferably stone-ground

¼ teaspoon kosher salt

¼ teaspoon baking soda

5 tablespoons (2½ ounces) unsalted butter with 82% butterfat, chilled, cut into ½-inch cubes

1 cup packed (6 ounces) dark brown cane sugar

Cinnamon sugar: 2 tablespoons granulated cane sugar mixed with ½ teaspoon ground cinnamon, ⅛ teaspoon ground cloves, and ¼ teaspoon kosher salt

Sylvester Graham, an American Presbyterian minister who championed whole-wheat flour and preached sexual restraint along with vegetarianism in the early 1800s, is believed to be the inventor of graham crackers. He would not have approved of the all-purpose flour in this recipe, but we suspect these crackers are better than the originals. Enjoy these treats alone, or pair them with marshmallows and chocolate to make s'mores (page 98).

If your brown sugar is lumpy, push it through a sieve before measuring it. Also, refrigerating the dough for at least 3 hours before rolling and baking helps to relax the gluten and blend the flavors.

Mix the dough

- Whisk the milk, vanilla extract, and honey together in a bowl. Set aside.

- Sift both flours, the salt, and the baking soda together into the bowl of a heavy-duty mixer fitted with the paddle attachment. Add the butter and beat on medium speed until the mixture looks like coarse meal. Beat in the brown sugar until no sugar clumps remain.

- With the mixer running on medium speed, add the milk mixture and beat until a smooth dough forms, 2 to 3 minutes.

- Turn the dough out onto a lightly floured work surface and pat it into a 5-inch square. Wrap it in plastic wrap and refrigerate for at least 3 hours or up to overnight.

Bake the crackers

- Preheat the oven to 350°F. Line the bottoms of two 12-by-18-inch sheet pans with parchment paper.

- On a lightly floured work surface, roll out the dough ⅛ inch thick. Using a ruler to guide you and a pizza cutter or a sharp knife, cut the dough in 2½-inch squares. You should have 30 squares. Reroll the scraps only once if necessary to yield that amount, using less flour on the work surface to prevent toughness. Put the squares on the prepared pans, spacing them ¼ inch apart. Sprinkle evenly with the cinnamon sugar.

- Bake on the middle shelves of the oven, rotating the pans 180 degrees halfway through the baking time, until browned on top, 15 to 18 minutes. Let cool completely on the pans on wire racks. Store in an airtight container for up to 2 weeks.

❋ Tahitian Vanilla Bean Marshmallows ❋

Old-fashioned candies are popular once again, and marshmallows are on the top of the list. Michael began making these on a whim, and soon Williams-Sonoma was ordering so many that Recchiuti Confections invested in an eighty-quart mixer to meet the demand.

These are puffs of sweetness on their own, or become s'mores when joined by Graham Crackers (page 96) and a piece of intense chocolate. Cut into smaller pieces, the marshmallows add lightness to Rocky Recchiuti Brownies (page 101).

You will need a 5-quart heavy-duty mixer to beat the thick mixture. If you can resist the temptation to eat them right away, the marshmallows will be firmer and easier to cut if left overnight at room temperature.

- Line the bottom of an 8-by-12-inch sheet pan with parchment paper and lightly coat the paper and the pan sides with flavorless vegetable oil.

- Put the gelatin in a small bowl. Add the water and stir. Set aside to soften.

- Combine 1 cup (7 ounces) of the sugar with the corn syrup in a large, heavy-bottomed pot. Use an unlined copper pot if you have one. Place over medium heat and cook, stirring occasionally with a wooden spoon, until the sugar melts. Then continue to cook, without stirring, until the mixture reaches 240°F on a candy thermometer. If any crystals form on the sides of the pan as the mixture heats, wash them down with a wet pastry brush.

- Meanwhile, put the egg whites in the bowl of a stand mixer fitted with the whip attachment. Scrape the seeds from the vanilla bean into the bowl.

- When the sugar syrup reaches 240°F, start to beat the egg whites on medium speed. When the whites form very soft peaks, add the remaining 1 cup (7 ounces) sugar and continue beating.

- When the sugar syrup reaches 250°F, remove it from the heat and stir in the softened gelatin. The syrup will foam up and triple in volume.

About 40 marshmallows

Flavorless vegetable oil for the pan

3³/₄ teaspoons (1½ envelopes) unflavored gelatin

3 tablespoons water

2 cups (14 ounces) granulated cane sugar, divided into halves

1½ cups (16 ounces by weight) light corn syrup

4 (5 ounces) extra-large egg whites, at room temperature

1 Tahitian vanilla bean, split horizontally

About 3 cups powdered cane sugar for finishing

continued next page . . .

- Switch the mixer to high speed and slowly pour the syrup into the beaten egg whites, aiming for the side of the bowl. The whites will almost double in volume. Reduce the speed to medium-high and beat until the whites (not the outside of the bowl) are lukewarm to the touch, about 114°F, about 15 minutes.

- Scrape the marshmallow mixture into the prepared pan and, using a small offset spatula, spread it evenly to the sides. Let cool completely at room temperature.

- To cut the marshmallows, sift about ½ cup of the powdered sugar onto a work surface in a rectangle the size of the sheet pan. Sift another 2 cups powdered sugar into a large bowl. Run a thin-bladed knife around the edge of the pan to loosen the marshmallow. Invert the pan onto the sugared surface to unmold, then lift off the pan and peel off the parchment paper. Sift about ½ cup powdered sugar evenly over the top. Using a ruler to guide you and a lightly oiled sharp knife, cut the marshmallow sheet into 1½-inch squares. It is easier if you use a pressing motion, rather than pull the knife. After cutting, toss the marshmallows, a few at a time, in the bowl of powdered sugar, coating them lightly.

- Store the marshmallows in an airtight container at room temperature, not in the refrigerator. They will keep for up to 1 month.

Variation

- If you have tempered chocolate on hand for another use, put some in a separate bowl and dip the marshmallows into the chocolate, covering half of each marshmallow. Place on a work surface, chocolate side up, until the chocolate sets.

❧ S'mores ❧

- Put a piece of chocolate on top of each graham cracker, and then top the chocolate with a marshmallow. Put the towers on a sheet pan. Run the pan under a preheated broiler until the marshmallows caramelize and the chocolate pieces melt, about 30 seconds. Top each tower with another graham cracker before serving, or serve open-faced.

❖ Fudge Brownies ❖

Not a cake, and not a candy, these dense squares are a bit of each. Their fudgelike texture comes from sugar, and the sweetness is offset by intense unsweetened chocolate, some melted into the batter and some left in chunks. They demand a high-quality chocolate to shine.

- Preheat the oven to 325°F. Line the bottom of an 8-inch square baking pan with parchment paper and liberally coat the paper and the pan sides with flavorless vegetable oil.

- Put 2½ ounces of the chocolate and the butter in a medium stainless-steel bowl and set over a pot of simmering water. Heat, stirring occasionally, until the chocolate and butter melt and are fully combined and the mixture is smooth. Lift the bowl from the pot. Set aside.

- Sift the flour and salt together into a bowl. In another bowl, combine the eggs and vanilla extract and whisk together by hand until blended. Whisk in the sugar.

- Whisk the egg mixture into the chocolate. Add the flour and the remaining 2½ ounces chocolate to the batter and, using a rubber spatula, mix well.

- Pour the batter into the prepared pan. Spread it evenly with a small offset spatula.

- Bake on the middle shelf of the oven until the top gives slightly to the touch and a skewer inserted into the center of the brownie comes out with some batter clinging to it, about 30 minutes. Let cool completely in the pan on a wire rack, then cover with plastic wrap and refrigerate until cold.

- Run a table knife around the edge of the pan to loosen the sides of the brownie, and then slide the brownie, still on the paper, onto a work surface. Using a ruler to guide you and a sharp knife, cut into sixteen 2-inch squares. Store in an airtight container in the refrigerator for up to 3 weeks.

16 brownies

Flavorless vegetable oil for the pan

5 ounces 100% unsweetened chocolate, coarsely chopped, divided into halves

8 tablespoons (4 ounces) unsalted butter with 82% butterfat, cut into 1-inch pieces

⅔ cup (3⅓ ounces) unbleached all-purpose flour

½ teaspoon kosher salt

3 (6 ounces) extra-large eggs, at room temperature

1 teaspoon pure vanilla extract, preferably Madagascar Bourbon

1¼ cups (9 ounces) granulated cane sugar

❧ ROCKY RECCHIUTI BROWNIES ❧

Save some homemade marshmallows (page 97) for topping these fanciful creations. When adding them to the batter, make sure they remain extended above the surface so that they will turn a toasty brown in the heat of the oven.

(page 97)

- Preheat the oven to 325°F. Line the bottom of an 8-inch square baking pan with parchment paper and liberally coat the paper and the pan sides with flavorless vegetable oil.

- Put 3 ounces of the chocolate and the butter in a medium stainless-steel bowl and set over a pot of simmering water. Heat, stirring occasionally, until the chocolate and butter melt and are fully combined and the mixture is smooth. Lift the bowl from the pot. Set aside.

- Sift the flour and salt together into a bowl. In another bowl, combine the eggs and vanilla extract and whisk together by hand until blended. Whisk in the sugar.

- Whisk the egg mixture into the chocolate. Add the flour and the remaining 2½ ounces chocolate to the batter and, using a rubber spatula, mix well. Then mix in the walnuts.

- Pour the batter into the prepared pan. Spread it evenly with a small offset spatula. Scatter the marshmallow pieces evenly over the surface and push them halfway into the batter. The tops should remain uncovered.

- Bake on the middle shelf of the oven until the marshmallows are browned and a skewer inserted into the center of the brownie sheet comes out with some batter clinging to it, about 45 minutes. Let cool completely in the pan on a wire rack, then cover with plastic wrap and refrigerate until cold.

- Run a table knife around the edge of the pan to loosen the sides of the brownie, and then slide the brownie, still on the paper, onto a work surface. Using a ruler to guide you and a sharp knife, cut into sixteen 2-inch squares. Store in an airtight container in the refrigerator for up to 3 weeks.

16 brownies

Flavorless vegetable oil for the pan

5½ ounces 100% unsweetened chocolate, coarsely chopped, divided

10 tablespoons (5 ounces) unsalted butter with 82% butterfat, cut into 1-inch slices

⅔ cup (3½ ounces) unbleached all-purpose flour

½ teaspoon kosher salt

3 (6 ounces) extra-large eggs, at room temperature

1 teaspoon pure vanilla extract, preferably Madagascar Bourbon

1⅓ cups (10 ounces) granulated cane sugar

⅓ cup (1½ ounces) walnut halves, roasted and roughly chopped

6 marshmallows, each 1½ inches square, cut into quarters

❧ Classic Ice-Cream Sandwiches ❧

12 sandwiches

THE CAKES

Flavorless vegetable oil for the pans

1 cup plus 2 tablespoons (5¾ ounces) unbleached all-purpose flour

⅓ cup plus 1 tablespoon (1½ ounces) unsweetened natural cocoa powder

½ teaspoon baking soda

¼ teaspoon kosher salt

⅔ cup (5¼ ounces) whole milk

1½ teaspoons pure vanilla extract, preferably Madagascar Bourbon

6 tablespoons (3 ounces) unsalted butter with 82% butterfat, at room temperature

¾ cup (5¼ ounces) granulated cane sugar

THE FILLING

1 quart just-churned ice cream, or purchased ice cream softened to a just-churned consistency

---

The thin, soft cake that forms these ice-cream sandwiches will remind you of your childhood, but will taste better than any of your recollections. You can make the sandwiches in a flash with purchased ice cream, but either the burnt caramel (page 166) or the cocoa nib (page 170) ice cream would elevate them to another realm.

Since the cakes go into the freezer for 45 minutes before assembly, time the churning of the ice cream accordingly. Work quickly when assembling the sandwich rectangle, especially if it's a hot day, or the ice cream will melt before you can slip the filled rectangle into the freezer. Make sure, too, that the tops of the cakes are facing outward on the sandwiches.

Bake the cakes

- Preheat the oven to 350°F. Dab a little flavorless vegetable oil on each of the 4 bottom corners of two 8-by-12-inch sheet pans, then line the bottoms with parchment paper. (The oil will anchor the paper.)

- Sift the flour, cocoa powder, baking soda, and salt together into a medium bowl. Measure the milk, and then add the vanilla extract to it.

- In a medium bowl, beat the butter with a rubber spatula until it is creamy. Beat in the sugar just until combined. Mix in the dry ingredients in 3 additions alternately with the wet ingredients in 2 additions. Be careful not to overmix.

- Divide the batter evenly between the 2 prepared pans and use a small offset spatula to spread it as evenly as possible.

- Bake on the middle shelves of the oven, rotating the pans 180 degrees halfway through the baking time, until slightly puffed and a skewer inserted into the center of each cake comes out clean, 10 to 12 minutes. Remove from the oven and immediately run the small offset spatula around the edges of the pans to loosen the cakes. Slide the cakes, still on the parchment paper, onto wire racks. Let cool completely.

Assemble the sandwiches

- Carefully return the baked cakes to one of the 8-by-12-inch sheet pans, stacking them with paper sides out and a sheet of parchment paper between them. Freeze them for 45 minutes to make them easier to handle.

- Line the bottom of another 8-by-12-inch sheet pan with parchment paper. Remove the cakes from the freezer. Place 1 cake, paper side up, in the sheet pan and carefully peel off the paper. Using a small offset spatula, evenly spread the ice cream over the cake, stopping ¼ inch from the edge on all sides.

- Remove the parchment paper from the bottom of the second cake. Place the cake, top side up, on a rimless cookie sheet. Holding the cookie sheet at an angle over the ice cream, carefully slide the cake onto the ice cream. Lightly press on the top cake to adhere it to the ice cream.

- Cover the pan with plastic wrap and freeze until the ice cream is solid, about 6 hours or up to overnight.

- To cut the rectangle into individual sandwiches, remove the pan from the freezer and remove the plastic wrap. Invert the rectangle onto a work surface, lift off the pan, and remove the parchment paper. Using a large, sharp knife, trim the edges of the rectangle so that they are even. Using a ruler to guide you, cut the rectangle into 12 equal pieces (each roughly 3 inches square) with the knife, dipping it into hot water and wiping it dry between each cut.

- Wrap the sandwiches individually in plastic wrap and keep them frozen until serving.

Variations

- After you have cut the rectangle into individual sandwiches, you can dress up each sandwich by rolling the ice-cream edges in finely chopped roasted or caramelized nuts, finely chopped caramelized cocoa nibs (see Caramelized Cocoa Nib White Chocolate Bark, page 140), or shaved chocolate before wrapping and freezing.

12 sandwiches

THE CAKES

Flavorless vegetable oil for the pan

2½ ounces 100% unsweetened chocolate, coarsely chopped

8 tablespoons (4 ounces) unsalted butter with 82% butterfat, cut into 1-inch pieces

⅔ cup (3⅓ ounces) unbleached all-purpose flour

½ teaspoon kosher salt

3 (6 ounces) extra-large eggs, at room temperature

1 teaspoon pure vanilla extract, preferably Madagascar Bourbon

1¼ cups (9 ounces) granulated cane sugar

THE FILLING

1 quart just-churned ice cream, or purchased ice cream softened to a just-churned consistency

The Fudge Brownies (page 99) can certainly stand on their own, but their dense texture is perfect to house a layer of ice cream. In this recipe, the brownie batter is made without the chocolate chunks and is baked into two thin layers. If you are a fan of bananas, make these sandwiches with Roasted Banana Ice Cream (page 169) for a real treat.

As with the classic sandwiches (page 102), you should churn the ice cream while the cakes are in the freezer for 45 minutes, and you need to work quickly when assembling the rectangle.

Bake the cakes

- Preheat the oven to 325°F. Dab a little flavorless vegetable oil on each of the 4 bottom corners of two 8-by-12-inch sheet pans, then line the bottoms with parchment paper. (The oil will anchor the paper.)

- Put the chocolate and butter in a medium stainless-steel bowl and set over a pot of simmering water. Heat, stirring occasionally, until the chocolate and butter melt and are fully combined and the mixture is smooth. Lift the bowl from the pot. Set aside.

- Sift the flour and salt together into a bowl. In another bowl, combine the eggs and vanilla extract and whisk together by hand until blended. Whisk in the sugar.

- Whisk the egg mixture into the chocolate. Add the flour to the batter and stir in with a rubber spatula.

- Divide the batter evenly between the 2 prepared pans and use a small offset spatula to spread it as evenly as possible.

- Bake on the middle shelves of the oven, rotating the pans 180 degrees halfway through the baking time, until the cakes start to pull away from the sides of the pans and a skewer inserted into the center of each one comes out clean, 18 to 20 minutes. Remove from the oven and immediately run a small offset spatula around the edges of the pans to loosen the cakes. Slide the cakes, still on the parchment paper, onto wire racks. Let cool completely.

Assemble the sandwiches

- Carefully return the baked cakes to one of the 8-by-12-inch sheet pans, stacking them with paper sides out and a sheet of parchment paper between them. Freeze them for 45 minutes to make them easier to handle.

- Line the bottom of another 8-by-12-inch sheet pan with parchment paper. Remove the cakes from the freezer. Place 1 cake, paper side up, in the sheet pan and carefully peel off the paper. Using a small offset spatula, evenly spread the ice cream over the cake, stopping ¼ inch from the edge on all sides.

- Remove the parchment paper from the bottom of the second cake. Place the cake, top side up, on a rimless cookie sheet. Holding the cookie sheet at an angle over the ice cream, carefully slide the cake onto the ice cream. Lightly press on the top cake to adhere it to the ice cream.

- Cover the pan with plastic wrap and freeze until the ice cream is solid, about 6 hours or up to overnight.

- To cut the rectangle into individual sandwiches, remove the pan from the freezer and remove the plastic wrap. Invert the rectangle onto a work surface, lift off the pan, and remove the parchment paper. Using a large, sharp knife, trim the edges of the rectangle so that they are even. Using a ruler to guide you, cut the rectangle into 12 pieces (each roughly 3 inches square) with the knife, dipping it into hot water and wiping it dry between each cut.

- Wrap the sandwiches individually in plastic wrap and keep them frozen until serving.

Variations

- After you have cut the rectangle into individual sandwiches, you can dress up each sandwich by rolling the ice-cream edges in finely chopped roasted or caramelized nuts, finely chopped caramelized cocoa nibs (see Caramelized Cocoa Nib White Chocolate Bark, page 140), or shaved chocolate before wrapping and freezing.

❋ Chocolate Shortbread Cookies with Truffle Cream Filling ❋

These dainty rounds are sandwiched with truffle cream made the old-fashioned way: by pouring hot cream over chopped chocolate. It creates a stiff filling that can support the top cookie in the sandwich.

Contrary to many recipes that call for creaming together butter and sugar until fluffy, this method instead beats these ingredients until they are just combined. Overmixing beats in excess air, resulting in cookies that spread too much in the oven. The dough needs to rest for at least 3 hours in the refrigerator, so you will need to plan ahead. The cookies can be baked up to 4 to 5 days in advance, however, and stored in an airtight container. Assemble the sandwiches shortly before serving and keep them in a cool place before taking them to the table.

Make the dough

- Sift the flour, cocoa powder, and salt together into a bowl. Set aside.

- Put the butter and sugar in the bowl of a stand mixer fitted with the paddle attachment. Beat on medium speed just until combined. Add the vanilla extract.

- Switch the mixer to low speed and add the dry ingredients in 3 additions, pulsing the mixer to incorporate each addition before adding the next one. The dough will look dry.

- Turn the dough out onto a lightly floured work surface. Knead a few times just until it comes together. Flatten into a disk, wrap in plastic wrap, and refrigerate until firm, at least 3 hours or up to 2 days.

Bake the cookies

- Preheat the oven to 325°F. Line the bottoms of two 12-by-18-inch sheet pans with parchment paper.

- Remove the dough from the refrigerator and unwrap it. On a lightly floured work surface, roll out the dough ⅛ inch thick. Using a 1½-inch round cookie cutter, cut out as many rounds as possible. Reroll the scraps only once, using less flour on the work surface to prevent toughness, and cut again. You should have 60 rounds in all. Place the rounds on the prepared pans, spacing them ½ inch apart.

30 cookies

THE COOKIES

1 cup (5 ounces) unbleached all-purpose flour

⅓ cup plus 1 tablespoon (1½ ounces) unsweetened natural cocoa powder

⅛ teaspoon kosher salt

8 tablespoons (4 ounces) unsalted butter with 82% butterfat, at room temperature

½ cup (3½ ounces) granulated cane sugar

¼ teaspoon pure vanilla extract, preferably Madagascar Bourbon

THE FILLING

4 ounces 65% chocolate, roughly chopped

⅓ cup (2½ ounces) heavy whipping cream

⅓ cup plus 1 tablespoon (1½ ounces) powdered cane sugar

2 tablespoons (1 ounce) unsalted butter with 82% butterfat, very soft (75°F°)

1½ teaspoons pure vanilla extract, preferably Madagascar Bourbon

Unsweetened natural cocoa powder for finishing cookies

continued next page . . .

- Bake on the middle shelves of the oven, rotating the pans 180 degrees halfway through the baking time, until the tops are lightly cracked and hold a slight indentation when pressed with a fingertip, about 10 minutes. Let cool completely on the pans on wire racks.

- Store in an airtight container at room temperature until you are ready to assemble the sandwiches.

Make the filling and assemble the cookies

- Put the chocolate in a medium bowl.

- Put the cream and powdered sugar in a small saucepan and bring to a simmer over medium heat. Cook at a simmer for 1 minute and remove from the heat.

- Pour the hot cream mixture over the chocolate. Whisk the mixture by hand until the chocolate melts. Whisk in the butter, and then the vanilla extract.

- Pour the truffle cream into a bowl, cover with plastic wrap so that the wrap is touching the surface, and refrigerate until the consistency of thick mayonnaise, 30 to 45 minutes.

- Arrange half of the cookies, bottom side up, on a sheet pan. Put the truffle cream into a pastry bag fitted with a 1/4-inch star tip and pipe a swirl of the cream onto the top of each cookie, distributing the cream evenly among them. Top each covered cookie with a second cookie, bottom side down, and press gently to adhere it to the truffle cream. Store in a cool place until serving.

- Just before serving, sift a dusting of cocoa powder on the tops of the cookies. Transfer to a serving plate.

❧ Triple-Chocolate Cookies ❧

Cocoa powder, milk chocolate, and dark chocolate give these cookies an intense chocolate taste. A dose of *fleur de sel* keeps them from being too sweet.

The dough is rolled into logs and refrigerated before being cut and baked, so make it at least 3 hours ahead. The dough may crumble a little as you cut the logs. If this happens, push each slice back together.

Make the dough

- Sift the flour, cocoa, and baking soda together into a bowl. Set aside.

- Put the butter in the bowl of a stand mixer fitted with the paddle attachment. Beat on medium speed until creamy. Add both sugars and the vanilla extract. Scrape the seeds from the vanilla bean into the bowl. Sprinkle the salt over the top. Beat on medium speed just until combined.

- Reduce the speed to low. Add the dry ingredients in 3 additions, pulsing the mixer to incorporate each addition before adding the next one. Pulse just until a crumbly dough forms. Add both chopped chocolates and mix on low speed just until incorporated.

- Turn the dough out onto a lightly floured work surface. Knead a few times to incorporate any crumbs.

- Divide the dough in half. Roll each half into a log about 1¼ inches in diameter and 12 inches long. As you roll, gently push the ends toward the center occasionally to prevent air pockets from forming and to keep the logs at an even thickness.

- Wrap the logs in plastic wrap and refrigerate until firm, at least 3 hours or up to 3 days.

Bake the cookies

- Preheat the oven to 325°F. Line the bottoms of two 12-by-18-inch sheet pans with parchment paper.

- Remove the logs from the refrigerator and unwrap them. Using a ruler to guide you and a sharp knife, cut each log into rounds ½ inch thick. If the dough crumbles as you cut it, reshape each slice. Place the rounds on the prepared pans, spacing them 1½ inches apart.

- Bake on the middle shelves of the oven, rotating the pans 180 degrees halfway through the baking time, until set but soft enough to hold a slight indentation when pressed with a fingertip, about 14 minutes. Let cool completely on the pans on wire racks.

- Store in an airtight container at room temperature for up to 1 week.

About 48 cookies

1⅓ cups (7 ounces) unbleached all-purpose flour

⅓ cup plus 1 tablespoon (1½ ounces) unsweetened natural cocoa powder

½ teaspoon baking soda

12 tablespoons (6 ounces) unsalted butter with 82% butterfat, at room temperature

½ cup (3½ ounces) granulated cane sugar

¾ cup (4½ ounces) dark brown cane sugar

½ teaspoon pure vanilla extract, preferably Madagascar Bourbon or Tahitian

½ Tahitian vanilla bean, split horizontally

½ teaspoon *fleur de sel* in fine grains

3 ounces 41% milk chocolate, roughly chopped

3 ounces 65% chocolate, roughly chopped

❖ Chocolate-Dipped Sesame Tuiles ❖

About 48 cookies

Flavorless vegetable oil for the pans

½ cup plus 1 tablespoon (2½ ounces) sesame seeds, preferrably unhulled

⅓ cup (2½ ounces) granulated cane sugar

⅓ cup (1¾ ounces) unbleached all-purpose flour

⅛ tablespoon kosher salt

2 (2½ ounces) extra-large egg whites, at room temperature

3 tablespoons (1½ ounces) unsalted butter with 82% butterfat, very soft (75°F)

About 8 ounces tempered 70% chocolate for coating cookies

Classic French *tuile* cookies definitely belong in the dessert realm. And so do these chocolate-dipped *tuiles*, although the addition of sesame seeds is a nod to the savory realm as well.

You can make the batter and bake it all or bake some and save some, refrigerated, to bake another day. It will keep for up to 1 week. Wait until you temper chocolate for another use to coat the cookies.

Bake the cookies

- Preheat the oven to 350°F. Line the bottoms of four 12-by-18-inch sheet pans with parchment paper. Lightly coat the paper with flavorless vegetable oil. Put a rolling pin on a work surface. If you have 2 rolling pins, ready both.

- Combine the sesame seeds, sugar, flour, and salt in a medium bowl and whisk by hand until combined. Mix—don't beat—the egg whites into the sesame seed mixture with a rubber spatula. Stir in the butter with the spatula until no streaks of butter remain.

- Measure 2 level teaspoons batter onto a prepared sheet pan. Using a small offset spatula, spread it into a round about 3½ inches in diameter. Repeat with the remaining batter, putting 8 rounds on each pan and leaving 1½ inches between the rounds.

- Bake the trays, one at a time, until the cookies are a uniform golden brown, 6 to 8 minutes. Remove from the oven and, while the cookies are still warm, run the offset spatula under each cookie and place it upside down on the rolling pin so that it curls around the pin. (You should be able to fit 5 cookies on a rolling pin, so by the time the sixth cookie is about to be draped over the pin, a few should be ready to be moved. Ideally, though, you will have 2 rolling pins.) If some of the cookies are not a uniform color, or if some cool too much and are no longer pliable, return them to the oven for another minute until evenly golden brown and again pliable.

- Leave the cookies on the rolling pin until they cool completely and have become brittle, a matter of seconds. Carefully lift them off and store them in an airtight container at room temperature until you are ready to dip them. They will keep well for up to 3 days.

Dip the cookies in chocolate

- You can store the cookies and dip them on a day when you have tempered chocolate for another use. Or, you can temper chocolate specifically to finish the cookies. (See the instructions for tempering chocolate on page 28.)

- Dip the convex (smooth) side of each cookie into the chocolate and then smooth the chocolate with a small offset spatula. Place on a work surface, chocolate side up, and let sit until the chocolate sets, about 30 minutes.

- Store in an airtight container in a cool place, not in the refrigerator. They will keep for up to 1 week.

❧ KEY LIME PEARS ❧

About 50 pieces

2 cups (14 ounces) granulated
cane sugar

1 ²⁄₃ cups (13 ounces) water

1 cup (8 ounces) Key lime juice
(about 30 limes)

3 medium Bartlett pears, green and
hard

About 12½ ounces tempered 65% to
70% chocolate for coating pears

The lime and pear flavors commingle in these treats, and a slow drying in the oven intensifies their flavor. The slices are then finished with a paper-thin coating of dark chocolate.

Key limes, which turn yellow when ripe and are very juicy, are small aromatic fruits with a more complex taste than the more familiar and larger green Persian limes stocked in most markets. Some supermarkets sell either fresh Key limes or their bottled juice (see Resources). If you can't find them, substitute the larger green limes. You will need only about 10 of the larger limes to yield the same amount of juice.

Steep the pears

- Put the sugar and water in a medium saucepan. Stir occasionally over medium heat until the sugar dissolves and the syrup starts to simmer, about 3 minutes.

- Add the lime juice, remove from the heat, and let cool to room temperature. Transfer to a large bowl.

- Using a mandoline or a V-Slicer, cut the pears lengthwise into slices ¹⁄₁₆ inch thick. Use the middle section of the pears, discarding the first 3 or 4 slices and the last ¼ inch of each pear. As each pear is cut, immediately submerge the slices in the lime-sugar syrup. Cover and refrigerate overnight or up to 4 days.

Dry the pears

- Preheat the oven to 225°F. Line the bottoms of three 12-by-18-inch sheet pans with parchment paper.

- Remove the sliced pears from the syrup and pat them dry with paper towels. Arrange the slices close together on the prepared pans. If your oven won't accommodate 3 pans, bake them in shifts.

- Bake the pear slices until they are completely dry and a medium brown, about 2 hours. To test, remove one and let it cool. It should be very crisp. If not, bake the slices a few minutes longer.

- Let cool completely at room temperature, then store in airtight containers. They will keep for up to 2 weeks.

Coat the pears with chocolate

- You can store the pears and dip them on a day when you have tempered chocolate for another use. Or, you can temper chocolate specifically to finish the pears. (See the instructions for tempering chocolate on page 28.) Line the bottoms of three 12-by-18-inch sheet pans with parchment paper.

- Hold one end of each pear slice in your hand and dip it into the chocolate, coating as much as possible. Place the covered slice on a prepared pan. Continue until all the slices are dipped. Leave them at room temperature until the chocolate sets, about 30 minutes.

- Store in an airtight container in a cool place, not in the refrigerator, for up to 2 weeks.

❈ DRIED-FRUIT CLUSTERS ❈

The mix of fruits, pistachios, and caramelized cocoa nibs is only a suggestion. Substitute your favorites for some or all of these ingredients, keeping the amounts and sizes of the fruits the same.

Use paper liners for miniature muffin cups for portioning out the clusters. They should measure 2 inches top diameter and 1 inch deep. See the instructions for tempering chocolate on page 28.

- Combine the dried fruits, caramelized cocoa nibs, pistachios, and salt together in a bowl. Stir to mix. Add the chocolate and stir until the fruits, nuts, and cocoa nibs clump together.

- Use a tablespoon to divide the clusters of chocolate-covered fruits and nuts evenly among paper liners for miniature muffin cups.

- Store in an airtight container in a cool, dry place, not in the refrigerator.

24 clusters

¾ cup (3¾ ounces) dried blueberries

¾ cup (3 ounces) dried pitted sour cherries

1 tablespoon (¼ ounce) dried cranberries

3 tablespoons (¾ ounce) caramelized cocoa nibs (see Caramelized Cocoa Nib White Chocolate Bark, page 140)

2 tablespoons (½ ounce) shelled green pistachios, roasted

¼ teaspoon kosher salt

½ cup (4¾ ounces by weight) tempered 65% chocolate

4 medium grapefruits or 6 large oranges

5 cups (35 ounces) granulated cane sugar

4¼ cups (34 ounces) water

⅔ cup (7 ounces by weight) light corn syrup

Slow cooking in sugar syrup preserves citrus peel indefinitely, and this recipe gives you ample amounts for myriad uses. Thin strips of dried grapefruit peel grace the tops of tarragon ganache squares (page 62) before they are dipped in chocolate, and pieces of dried orange peel give a citrus note to dark chocolate bark (page 137). Either peel, cut into long strips, dried, and dusted in granulated cane sugar, is a welcome in a selection of chocolates. Chopped peel can be sprinkled over ice cream or added to baked goods. The orange peel is even more delicious if it's dipped in chocolate.

Correctly separating the pulp from the peel is important. Many recipes for candied peel advise removing all the pith, but if you leave about half its thickness, it prevents the candied strips from becoming too hard. To make the recipe less time-consuming, blanch the peel one day and cook it in the syrup on another day. Michael prefers Ruby Red grapefruits and Valencia oranges.

Peel and blanch the fruits

- The method is the same for either grapefruits or oranges. Cut each fruit into sixths through the stem end. Scrape off the pulp and reserve for another use. Leave the pith in place.

- The peels are blanched 3 times. Fill a large saucepan with water and bring it to a boil. Have a large bowl of ice water ready. Add the peels to the boiling water and bring the water back to a boil. Pour the peels and water into a sieve, and then put the peels in the ice water. Refill the saucepan with water and bring the water to a boil. Again, add the peels to the boiling water and return the water to a boil. Drain the peels and plunge them into the ice water (you may need to replenish some of the ice). Repeat the blanching and ice-water bath one more time.

- While you are waiting for the water to boil for the third blanching, remove about half of the thickness of the pith from each piece of peel. The outer rind should not be exposed on the pith side. A good tool to use is a flexible knife, such as a fillet knife.

Candy the peels

- Stir the sugar, water, and corn syrup together in a large saucepan. Place over medium heat and bring to a boil, stirring to dissolve the sugar. Meanwhile, cut 2 rounds of parchment paper slightly larger than the diameter of the pan. When the sugar syrup is boiling, add the blanched peel and bring back to a simmer. Cover the peels with a double layer of parchment paper to keep it submerged. Adjust the heat to maintain a simmer and cook until the peel looks translucent and the pith is soft, about 1 hour and 20 minutes. The temperature of the syrup will be about 220°F.

- Remove from the heat and let the peels cool in the syrup, with the parchment paper in place and undisturbed, at room temperature overnight.

- The next day, transfer the peels and syrup to a container with a tight-fitting lid and store in the refrigerator. The peels will keep indefinitely.

Note

- The corn syrup should prevent crystallization of the solution, but if the syrup does crystallize, remove the peels and wash off the crystallized sugar. Reheat the syrup over medium heat to a simmer, add the peels, and bring to a boil. Remove from the heat, cover with parchment paper as you did when you were simmering the peels, and let cool in the syrup, undisturbed, at room temperature overnight. Refrigerate again in a closed container.

Variations

- You can use the candied citrus peels just as they are for the uses described in the recipe introduction, but if you want to make them the star of the show, here are two possibilities.

Dust the peels in granulated sugar

- Remove the peels from the syrup and rinse off the syrup under cool water. Cut the pieces lengthwise into ¼-inch-wide strips. Put a wire rack on a sheet pan, and arrange the strips on the rack. Leave them at room temperature overnight, or until they are dry.

- Place granulated cane sugar in a bowl. Add the dried peel, a few strips at a time, and toss to coat evenly. Store in an airtight container in a cool, dry place, not in the refrigerator.

Dip the peels in chocolate

- Dry and cut the peels as described for dusting with granulated sugar, but don't toss them in the sugar. On a day when you have tempered chocolate for another use, use the leftover tempered chocolate to dip the candied peel strips. Hold one end of each strip with your fingers and dip half the strip into the chocolate. Put the strips on a parchment-lined sheet pan until the chocolate sets, about 30 minutes. Store in an airtight container in a cool, dry place, not in the refrigerator.

❦ Peanut Butter Pucks ❦

18 pucks

FOR THE PAPER LINERS

About 5 ounces tempered 65% to
70% chocolate

FOR THE FILLING

5 ounces 41% milk chocolate, finely
chopped

⅓ cup plus 2 tablespoons (4 ounces
by weight) smooth peanut butter, at
room temperature

Fleur de sel in fine grains

Here is Michael's version of an old-time favorite. Quality chocolate makes the difference. Use a smooth peanut butter made from roasted nuts and without added salt or sugar.

When you have tempered chocolate for another use, use what is left to paint paper muffin-cup liners with the chocolate.

Paint the muffin-cup liners

- If you are not using tempered chocolate left over from another use, temper the chocolate according to the instructions on page 28. Have ready 36 paper liners for miniature muffin cups. The liners should measure 2 inches top diameter and 1 inch deep. Stack 2 liners together to make a sturdier cup. Then, using a small, natural-bristle brush, evenly spread the tempered chocolate inside each pair of stacked cups. Let sit until the chocolate sets, about 20 minutes. If you can see through the chocolate after it sets, add another thin layer of chocolate, especially around the top.

- Set the coated cups aside on a sheet pan until you are ready to fill them.

Make the filling and fill the cups

- Put the chocolate in a medium stainless-steel bowl and set the bowl over a pot of simmering water. Heat, stirring occasionally, until the chocolate melts and registers no higher than 112°F on an instant-read thermometer. Lift the bowl from the pot.

- While the chocolate is melting, stir the peanut butter with a rubber spatula to distribute any oil that may have separated. When the chocolate is ready, mix the peanut butter into the chocolate with the spatula. Check the temperature; it should not exceed 85°F. Let the filling cool if it is too hot.

- Using a teaspoon, fill each chocolate-coated cup about two-thirds full with the filling. Refrigerate the cups until the filling is almost set, about 20 minutes. Sprinkle the tops with a few grains of *fleur de sel* and return to the refrigerator until the filling has completely set, about 20 minutes longer.

- When the filling has set completely, carefully peel off the paper from each cup. Store in an airtight container in the refrigerator for up to 2 weeks. Bring to room temperature before serving.

⋇ CHOCOLATE-COVERED CARAMELIZED HAZELNUTS ⋇

Sugar-coated nuts have a long history in the world of confectionery. Early candy makers took pride in their ability to control the addition of sugar syrup to a revolving pan of nuts, covering them in successive thin, uniform coatings. Steam-heated revolving pans, developed in the second half of the nineteenth century, made the work less laborious.

This recipe is a simple version of the original technique, with one important difference that makes these nuts even more delicious: a layer of chocolate covers the caramelized sugar that surrounds the nuts.

See the instructions for tempering chocolate on page 28.

Roast and skin the hazelnuts

- Preheat the oven to 350°F. Line the bottom of a sheet pan with parchment paper.

- Spread the hazelnuts on the prepared pan in a single layer. Roast the nuts until the skins start to darken and shrivel, about 8 minutes.

- Remove the nuts from the oven. As soon as they are cool enough to handle, rub them in batches in a kitchen towel to remove the skins. Not every bit will come off.

Caramelize the nuts

- Use only whole nuts, not broken pieces. Put a piece of parchment paper or a nonstick baking liner on a work surface. Measure the sugar and butter and put both of them next to the stove.

- Put the nuts in a medium heavy-bottomed pot. Use an unlined copper pot if you have one. Place over medium-high heat and cook, stirring constantly with a wooden spoon, for 1 minute to heat the nuts.

- Add the sugar to the nuts and continue to cook, stirring constantly with the wooden spoon, until the sugar liquefies and coats the nuts. If they start to smoke, reduce the heat. When only a few specks of sugar remain unmelted, remove from the heat and add the butter. Stir until the nuts glisten and start to separate from one another.

- Scrape the nuts onto the parchment paper or baking liner and separate them into individual pieces as best as you can. When they are cool enough to handle, carefully break apart any that are stuck together.

- Let the nuts cool to room temperature.

continued next page . . .

About 11 ounces

2 cups (8 ounces) whole hazelnuts

¼ cup (1 ¾ ounces) granulated cane sugar

2 teaspoons (⅓ ounce) unsalted butter with 82% butterfat

½ cup (2 ounces) unsweetened natural cocoa powder

½ cup (4 ¾ ounces by weight) tempered 65% to 70% chocolate

Coat the nuts with chocolate

- Chill a large metal bowl in the refrigerator for at least 20 minutes. Line the bottom of a large sheet pan with parchment paper. Sift the cocoa powder into a medium bowl.

- Put the caramelized nuts in the chilled bowl. Add the tempered chocolate and stir to coat the nuts with the chocolate. When the chocolate has almost set, after about 5 minutes, sift about half of the cocoa powder onto the nuts. Stir until the nuts start to separate, and then toss them with your hands to separate them into individual pieces. Add more cocoa powder if needed to separate them completely. You may have cocoa powder left over.

- Put the nuts in a sieve, shake them to remove any excess cocoa powder, and then spread them in a single layer on the prepared pan.

- When the chocolate has set, store the nuts in an airtight container in a cool, dry place, not in the refrigerator, for up to 2 weeks.

❧ Chocolate-Covered Caramelized Cashews ❧

About 11 ounces

1½ cups (7¼ ounces) whole cashews

⅓ cup (2½ ounces) granulated cane sugar

2 teaspoons (⅓ ounce) unsalted butter with 82% butterfat

½ cup (2 ounces) unsweetened natural cocoa powder

½ cup (4¾ ounces by weight) tempered 65% to 70% chocolate

This recipe is a variation of the recipe for Chocolate-Covered Caramelized Hazelnuts (page 117), but because cashews have a less pronounced taste, a little more sugar is used to make the caramel coating. See the instructions for tempering chocolate on page 28.

Roast and caramelize the cashews

- Preheat the oven to 350°F. Line the bottom of a sheet pan with parchment paper.

- Use only whole cashews, not broken pieces. Spread them on the prepared pan in a single layer. Roast the nuts until they are medium brown, about 12 minutes.

- While the nuts are roasting, put a piece of parchment paper or a nonstick baking liner on a work surface. Measure the sugar and butter and put both of them next to the stove.

- As soon as the nuts are roasted, place a medium heavy-bottomed pot over medium-high heat. Use an unlined copper pot if you have one. When the pot is hot—test by flicking a drop of water into the pan; it should sizzle and dance across the bottom—immediately add the hot nuts and the sugar. Cook, stirring constantly with a wooden spoon, until the sugar liquefies and coats the nuts. If they start to smoke, reduce the heat. When only a few specks of sugar remain unmelted, remove from the heat and add the butter. Stir until the nuts glisten and start to separate from one another.

- Scrape the nuts onto the parchment paper or baking liner and separate them into individual pieces as best as you can. When they are cool enough to handle, carefully break apart any that are stuck together.

- Let the nuts cool to room temperature.

Coat the nuts with chocolate

- Chill a large metal bowl in the refrigerator for at least 20 minutes. Line the bottom of a large sheet pan with parchment paper. Sift the cocoa powder into a medium bowl.

- Put the caramelized nuts in the chilled bowl. Add the tempered chocolate and stir to coat the nuts with the chocolate. When the chocolate has almost set, after about 5 minutes, sift about half of the cocoa powder onto the nuts. Stir until the nuts start to separate, and then toss them with your hands to separate them into individual pieces. Add more cocoa powder if needed to separate them completely. You may have cocoa powder left over.

- Put the nuts in a sieve, shake them to remove any excess cocoa powder, and then spread them in a single layer on the prepared pan.

- When the chocolate has set, store the nuts in an airtight container in a cool, dry place, not in the refrigerator, for up to 2 weeks.

Variation

- Use whole blanched almonds in place of the cashews. Reduce the sugar to ¼ cup (1¾ ounces).

15 pies

THE PIES

2 cups (10 ounces) unbleached all-purpose flour

⅔ cup (2½ ounces) unsweetened natural cocoa powder

¼ teaspoon kosher salt

1 teaspoon baking soda

1 tablespoon instant espresso powder dissolved in ½ cup (4 ounces) boiling water

½ cup (4 ounces) flavorless vegetable oil

⅔ cup (5 ounces) whole milk

1 cup (7 ounces) granulated cane sugar

1 (2 ounces) extra-large egg, at room temperature

1 cup (6 ounces) roughly chopped candied orange peel (see Candied Citrus Peel, page 114)

THE FILLING

1½ cups (12 ounces) heavy whipping cream

½ Tahitian vanilla bean, split horizontally

½ teaspoon pure vanilla extract, either Madagascar Bourbon or Tahitian

1 tablespoon plus 1 teaspoon powdered cane sugar

One of the jobs Michael had during his varied career was running a restaurant in Lancaster, Pennsylvania, in the heart of the Amish country. He became fascinated with the whoopie pies available at every country farm stand. Each had its special twist, slight variations in the texture or taste. Michael went on a mission to taste as many as possible, and after testing many recipes, he settled on this one.

The pies can be made 1 week ahead and stored in an airtight container at room temperature. Fill them and serve them on the same day. Make the candied orange peel at least 1 day ahead.

Bake the pies

- Preheat the oven to 325°F. Line the bottoms of two 12-by-18-inch sheet pans with parchment paper.

- Sift the flour, cocoa powder, and salt together into a bowl. Stir the baking soda into the dissolved instant espresso in another bowl and then stir in the oil and milk.

- Combine the sugar and egg in a medium bowl and whisk together by hand. Whisk in the flour mixture in 2 additions, alternately with the coffee mixture in 1 addition. Fold in the orange peel with a rubber spatula.

- Drop the batter by heaping tablespoonfuls onto the prepared pans, spacing them 2 inches apart. You should have 30 pies in all.

- Bake on the middle shelves of the oven, rotating the pans 180 degrees halfway through the baking time, until puffed and set but soft enough to hold a slight indentation when pressed with a fingertip, 10 to 12 minutes. Let cool completely on the pans on wire racks.

- Store in an airtight container at room temperature until you are ready to assemble the pies.

Make the filling and assemble the pies

- Arrange half of the pies, bottom side up, on a sheet pan.

- Put the cream in the bowl of a stand mixer fitted with the whip attachment. Scrape the seeds from the vanilla bean into the cream. Add the vanilla extract and sugar. Beat the cream on medium speed until medium-stiff peaks form.

- Put the cream into a pastry bag fitted with a ⅜-inch star tip. Pipe a swirl of the cream onto the top of each pie, distributing the cream evenly among them. Top each covered pie with a second pie, bottom side down, and press gently to adhere it to the cream.

- Store in a cool place until serving.

❧ Devil's Food Cupcakes with White Chocolate–Espresso Topping ❧

The rich brown hue of these cupcakes tells you that they will taste intensely of chocolate even before the first bite. The surprise might be the orange flavor that comes from the addition of orange zest in the batter. The espresso in the topping adds a third dimension.

Use a Microplane grater to zest the lemon. The cupcakes are best when served the same day they are made.

Bake the cupcakes

- Preheat the oven to 325°F. Line 12 standard muffin cups (2½ inches top diameter, 1¼ inches deep) with paper liners.

- Sift the flour, cocoa powder, salt, baking powder, baking soda, and sugar together into a medium bowl.

- Combine the egg, milk, oil, vanilla extract, and dissolved espresso powder in a medium bowl and whisk by hand until well mixed. Finely grate the zest from the orange directly into the bowl. Pour the wet ingredients into the dry ingredients and whisk to combine.

- Using a tablespoon, divide the batter evenly among the prepared muffin cups, filling them about half full.

- Bake on the middle shelf of the oven until the cupcakes are puffed and feel springy to the touch, 15 to 20 minutes. Let cool completely in the pan on a wire rack. When cool, remove the cupcakes, still in their paper liners, from the muffin cups.

Make the topping and finish the cupcakes

- Put the chocolate in a medium bowl.

- Whisk the espresso powder into the cream in a small saucepan and bring to a boil over medium heat. Pour the hot cream over the chocolate and whisk until it is melted.

- Put the bowl of topping in an ice-water bath and stir occasionally until the chocolate cools to 45°F, 15 to 20 minutes.

- When the topping has cooled, whisk it by hand until it is the consistency of soft ice cream.

- Put the topping into a pastry bag fitted with a ³⁄₈-inch star tip. Pipe a swirl on the top center of each cupcake, distributing the topping evenly among them.

- Store in a cool place until serving. Just before serving, sift a dusting of cocoa powder over the topping.

12 cupcakes

THE CUPCAKES

1 cup (5 ounces) unbleached all-purpose flour

⅓ cup (1¼ ounces) unsweetened natural cocoa powder

½ teaspoon kosher salt

½ teaspoon baking powder

½ teaspoon baking soda

1 cup (3½ ounces) granulated cane sugar

1 (2 ounces) extra-large egg

½ cup (4 ounces) whole milk

¼ cup (2 ounces) flavorless vegetable oil

½ teaspoon pure vanilla extract, preferably Madagascar Bourbon

1 tablespoon espresso powder dissolved in ½ cup (4 ounces) boiling water

1 orange

THE TOPPING

2¾ ounces white chocolate, finely chopped

1 tablespoon instant espresso powder

½ cup plus 1 tablespoon (4⅓ ounces) heavy whipping cream

Unsweetened natural cocoa powder for dusting the finished cupcakes

❧ White Cupcakes with Truffle Cream Topping ❧

12 cupcakes

THE CUPCAKES

1½ cups (7½ ounces) unbleached all-purpose flour

1 teaspoon baking powder

½ teaspoon baking soda

¼ teaspoon kosher salt

1 cup (8 ounces) crème fraîche, at room temperature

2 (4 ounces) extra-large eggs, at room temperature

1 teaspoon pure vanilla extract, preferably Madagascar Bourbon

6 tablespoons (3 ounces) unsalted butter with 82% butterfat, at room temperature

¾ cup (5¼ ounces) granulated cane sugar

THE TOPPING

8 ounces 65% chocolate, coarsely chopped

⅔ cup (5 ounces) heavy whipping cream

⅔ cup plus 2 tablespoons (3 ounces) powdered cane sugar

4 tablespoons (2 ounces) unsalted butter with 82% butterfat, very soft (75°F)

1 tablespoon pure vanilla extract, preferably Madagascar Bourbon

These tender cupcakes scented with vanilla are topped with a rich truffle filling, so chocolate lovers can have their cake and chocolate, too. The topping is a double recipe of the truffle cream filling for the chocolate shortbread cookies (page 107), but it is whipped to a fluffy lightness before being piped onto the cupcakes.

Like the other cupcakes in this chapter, these are best when served the same day they are made.

Bake the cupcakes

- Preheat the oven to 325°F. Line 12 standard muffin cups (2½ inches top diameter and 1¼ inches deep) with paper liners.

- Sift the flour, baking powder, baking soda, and salt together into a medium bowl.

- Combine the crème fraîche, eggs, and vanilla extract in a medium bowl and whisk by hand until well mixed.

- Put the butter in the bowl of a stand mixer fitted with the paddle attachment. Beat on medium speed until the butter is creamy. Add the granulated sugar and beat until fluffy and pale.

- Switch the mixer to low speed. Add the dry ingredients in 3 additions, alternating with the wet ingredients in 2 additions.

- Using a tablespoon, divide the batter evenly among the muffin cups, filling them about two-thirds full.

- Bake on the middle shelf of the oven until the cupcakes are puffed, lightly browned, slightly cracked on top, and a skewer inserted into the center of one comes out clean, 15 to 20 minutes. Let cool completely in the pan on a rack. When cool, remove the cupcakes, still in their paper liners, from the muffin cups.

Make the topping and finish the cupcakes

- Put the chocolate in a medium bowl.

- Put the cream and powdered sugar in a small saucepan and bring to a simmer over medium heat. Cook at a simmer for 1 minute and remove from the heat.

- Pour the hot cream mixture over the chocolate. Whisk the mixture by hand until the chocolate melts. Whisk in the butter, and then the vanilla extract.

- Pour into a bowl, cover with plastic wrap so that the wrap is touching the surface, and refrigerate until it is 70°F. This will probably take 30 to 40 minutes, but check after 20 minutes.

- When the cream is at the correct temperature, put it into the bowl of the stand mixer fitted with the whip attachment. Beat on high speed until the mixture is lighter in color and less dense.

- Put the topping into a pastry bag fitted with a ⅜-inch star tip. Pipe a swirl on the top center of each cupcake, distributing the topping evenly among them.

- Store in a cool place until serving.

12 cupcakes

THE CUPCAKES

2 cups plus 2 tablespoons (10²/₃ ounces) unbleached all-purpose flour

1½ teaspoons baking soda

1 teaspoon ground cinnamon

2 teaspoons ground ginger

1½ teaspoons kosher salt

1 (2 ounces) extra-large egg

½ cup (4³/₄ ounces by weight) dark molasses

½ cup (3½ ounces) granulated cane sugar

½ cup (4 ounces) flavorless vegetable oil

½ cup (4 ounces) boiling water

Lemon glaze: ¼ cup (2 ounces) fresh lemon juice and ¾ cup (2²/₃ ounces) powdered cane sugar

THE TOPPING

Lemon syrup: ¼ cup plus 2 tablespoons (3 ounces) fresh lemon juice; 1 tablespoon plus 1 teaspoon granulated cane sugar; ½ Tahitian vanilla bean, split horizontally; and ½ lemon

3³/₄ ounces white chocolate, very finely chopped

3 tablespoons (1½ ounces) heavy whipping cream

8 tablespoons (4 ounces) unsalted butter with 82% butterfat, at room temperature

1 lemon

Michael learned this recipe from a British chef who took great pride in his ginger cakes, as he called them. The chef always knew when Michael didn't bring the water to a boil; the texture of the cakes wasn't quite right. The spicy cupcakes are doused with lemon syrup to keep them moist. There is also lemon syrup in the topping, which tempers the sweetness of the white chocolate.

Use a Microplane grater to zest the lemon. Serve the cupcakes the day they are made.

Bake the cupcakes

- Preheat the oven to 325°F. Line 12 standard muffin cups (2½ inches top diameter and 1¼ inches deep) with paper liners.

- Sift the flour, baking soda, cinnamon, ginger, and salt together into a medium bowl. Set aside.

- Combine the egg, molasses, granulated sugar, and oil in a medium bowl and whisk by hand until well mixed. Whisk in the boiling water. Pour the wet ingredients into the dry ingredients and whisk to combine.

- Using a tablespoon, divide the batter evenly among the prepared muffin cups, filling them about half full.

- Bake on the middle shelf of the oven until the cupcakes are puffed and a skewer inserted into the center of one comes out clean, about 25 minutes.

- While the cupcakes are baking, make the lemon glaze: whisk the lemon juice and powdered sugar together until smooth.

- When the cupcakes are ready, remove them from the oven and immediately poke 4 evenly spaced holes in the top of each cupcake with a skewer. Spoon the lemon glaze evenly over the cupcakes, waiting until the glaze is absorbed before adding more. It will seem like too much, but use it all.

- Let the cupcakes cool completely in the pan on a wire rack. When cool, remove the cupcakes, still in their paper liners, from the muffin cups.

Make the topping and finish the cupcakes

- Make the lemon syrup: Put the lemon juice and granulated sugar in a small saucepan. Scrape the seeds from the vanilla bean into the pan. Finely grate the zest from the ½ lemon directly into the pan. Bring to a boil over medium heat, stirring to dissolve the sugar. Boil until the syrup is reduced by half—3 tablespoons—about 3 minutes. Pour the syrup into a small bowl and refrigerate it until it cools to 70°F.

- Put the chocolate in the bowl of a stand mixer fitted with the whip attachment. Put the cream in a saucepan and bring to a boil over medium heat. Pour the hot cream over the chocolate and beat on high speed until the chocolate melts and the mixture is smooth, about 2 minutes.

- Beat in the butter in 3 equal additions on medium speed until blended. Switch the mixer to high speed and beat until the topping is pale, fluffy, and doubled in volume, about 4 minutes.

- Reduce the speed to medium and beat in the cooled lemon syrup. If the topping is too runny to pipe, cover and chill in the refrigerator to make it firmer.

- Put the topping into a pastry bag fitted with a ⅜-inch star tip. Pipe a swirl on the top center of each cupcake, distributing the topping evenly among them. Garnish each cupcake with lemon zest, grating the zest from the lemon directly onto the cupcakes.

- Store in a cool place until serving.

❧ Burnt Caramel Pots de Crème ❧

12 servings

¾ cup (5¼ ounces) granulated cane sugar

2 tablespoons (1 ounce) water

¾ cup (6 ounces) whole milk

2 cups (16 ounces) heavy whipping cream

5 (3¾ ounces) extra-large egg yolks

2½ ounces 41% milk chocolate, finely chopped

Because a little of these rich custards goes a long way, bake them in espresso cups and bring them to the table to end a meal. They can be made a day ahead and refrigerated; allow them to come to room temperature before serving.

- Put the sugar and water in a medium heavy-bottomed pot. Use an unlined copper pan if you have one. Stir to mix the water and sugar. Place over medium heat and cook, stirring occasionally with a wooden spoon, until the sugar melts. Then continue to cook, without stirring, until the sugar turns dark amber, 4 to 5 minutes. To check the color, dab a small amount of the syrup on a white plate. If any crystals form on the sides of the pan as the sugar darkens, wash them down with a wet pastry brush.

- While the sugar is cooking, combine the milk and cream in a saucepan and bring to a boil over medium heat.

- When the sugar is the correct shade, remove the pan from the heat and put a sieve or splatter guard over it. Wearing an oven mitt, slowly pour the hot cream into the sugar syrup a little at a time. The mixture will sputter and foam. Be careful, as it is very hot. When the mixture stops bubbling, whisk it to incorporate any caramel stuck to the bottom.

- Place the egg yolks in a medium bowl and whisk by hand until blended. Whisk about ½ cup of the caramel mixture into the yolks to warm them gradually. Whisk in another 1 cup, and then whisk in the rest. Add the chocolate and whisk until it melts.

- Strain the custard through a fine-mesh sieve into a bowl. Spoon the custard into twelve 2½-ounce espresso cups, filling them three-fourths full. Let the custard cool to room temperature.

- Preheat the oven to 300°F. Bring a large teakettle of water to a simmer.

- Put the cups in a large baking pan. Pour the hot water into the baking pan to reach halfway up the sides of the cups. Cover the pan with aluminum foil.

- Bake on the middle shelf of the oven until the tops are set but the entire custard jiggles when a cup is moved, about 25 minutes. Immediately remove the cups from the hot water. Let cool to room temperature.

- Cover each cup and refrigerate for at least 6 hours or up to overnight. Bring to room temperature before serving.

❧ Double–Dark Chocolate Soufflés ❧

8 individual soufflés

THE MOLDS

About 4 teaspoons (²/₃ ounce) unsalted butter with 82% butterfat, very soft (75°F)

1 tablespoon plus 2 teaspoons (³/₄ ounce) granulated cane sugar

1½ ounces 70% chocolate, grated

THE SOUFFLÉS

2¼ cups (9 ounces) unsweetened natural cocoa powder

3 cups water

2 Tahitian vanilla beans, split horizontally

3 ounces 70% chocolate, grated

4 (5 ounces) extra-large egg whites, at room temperature

Pinch of kosher salt

¾ cup (5¼ ounces) granulated cane sugar

The large amount of cocoa powder in this recipe is responsible for the richness of the soufflés. And as if that isn't enough, 70% chocolate is folded into the batter. When Michael made this recipe in his pastry-chef days, he stood the chocolate batons normally used for *pains au chocolat* in the soufflés just before baking them. This recipe uses grated chocolate instead.

You can prepare the molds and make the chocolate base up to 6 hours ahead; reheat the base over simmering water before folding in the egg whites.

Line the molds

- Coat the bottoms and sides of eight 5-ounce individual soufflé molds with the butter.

- Mix the sugar and chocolate together in a bowl. Divide the mixture evenly among the molds, and then tilt and rotate the molds to coat the bottoms and sides fully and evenly. Refrigerate the molds while you prepare the soufflé base.

Bake the soufflés

- Preheat the oven to 350°F. Sift the cocoa powder into a bowl.

- Put the water in a medium saucepan. Scrape the vanilla seeds from the beans into the pan and then add the beans. Bring the water to a boil over medium heat and remove from the heat. Cover the pan with plastic wrap and let steep for 5 minutes. Take out the beans and bring the water back to a simmer over medium heat.

- Whisk about half of the cocoa powder into the water. After it is absorbed, whisk in the rest of the cocoa powder. Place over medium heat and cook, whisking constantly, until the base is the consistency of mayonnaise, 4 to 5 minutes. Remove from the heat.

- Put the egg whites and salt in the bowl of a stand mixer fitted with the whip attachment. Beat on medium speed until they start to froth and then add about one-third of the sugar. When the whites are opaque and start to increase in volume, add another one-third of the sugar. When they start to become stiff, increase the speed to high and add the rest of the sugar. Beat until the whites start to lose their shine but still look wet. They will hang in medium-stiff peaks when the whip is lifted from the bowl.

- Transfer the cocoa base to a large bowl. Fold about one-third of the whites into the base with a rubber spatula. Fold in the rest of the whites just until no white streaks remain.

- Distribute the mixture evenly among the prepared molds, filling them level with the top. Put the molds on a sheet pan.

- Bake on the middle shelf of the oven until the soufflés rise about 1 inch above the rim of the molds and have a crust on top, about 20 minutes. They will be wobbly.

- Transfer them to serving plates and take them to the table immediately.

Variation

- Just before serving, pierce the cap of each soufflé and spoon a tablespoon of Vanilla Bean Ice Cream (page 172) into the center.

AN AMERICAN IN PARIS

The French take their chocolate seriously, so much so that there are at least two chocolate clubs in Paris whose members meet regularly to taste confectioners' wares. As a young girl, Danielle Monteaux ate chocolate every day after school at a nearby shop. This long-standing passion eventually prompted her to organize Le Club du Chocolat aux Palais in 1991. Twenty-five people, most of them her colleagues in the legal world (she is a lawyer), attended the first meeting, where a nutrition expert discussed the therapeutic virtues of chocolate. Future meetings covered other topics, but most included a chocolate tasting, either alone or paired with wine or spirits.

In keeping with the double entendre of *palais*, which means both "palace" and "palate," the group often met in palaces or other prestigious places, and not only in Paris. They traveled

to other chocolate-prominent cities, such as Bayonne and to Tain L'Hermitage, the home of Valrhona. Although today some club members are professional chocolatiers, most still don't work in the chocolate world. Admission to the club is not a casual thing. To qualify for membership, applicants must write a letter describing their passion for chocolate and have two current members vouch for that passion. Only then will they be invited to join.

A mutual friend introduced Michael to Danielle. When she tasted his chocolates, she immediately invited him to present them at a tasting in Paris. He is the first American confectioner to be invited in the club's thirteen-year history. A mid-October date was set. Michael pondered his repertoire, deciding which chocolates to take. He wanted the selection to reflect his penchant for bold flavors and unusual combinations. After some thought, he chose honeycomb malt, cardamom nougat, Key lime pears, tarragon grapefruit, and mint tea. He added small bars of single varietal chocolates that he uses as a base for the confections.

The tasting was held in the Salon Récamier in the Hotel Westminster, not far from the fashionable Place Vendôme. Although not a palace room, it certainly looks like one. Relief panels and mirrors decorate the walls, crystal chandeliers hang from the tall ceilings, and plush floral carpeting covers the floor. Tablecloths were draped over six round tables, each of which sat ten. A tray of chocolates and bottles of mineral water were in the center of each table. A brochure describing the chocolates and a water glass was placed at each seat.

Club members, including two prominent Parisian *chocolatiers*, arrived in small groups and took

seats. Most were well dressed and middle-aged, with an even mix of men and women. When the room was full, Danielle introduced Michael in glowing terms, praising his inventiveness and skill. Michael thanked everyone and then the group got down to business. As people tasted, Michael described the chocolates as well as his philosophy of long infusions and burnt caramel. He stopped after every few sentences to allow a translation into French.

People wore pensive expressions and murmured among themselves as they tasted. Many took notes. Forty minutes into the event, the room was overflowing, but people were still arriving, so they huddled in the back of the room and out in the hallway, sampling from trays of chocolates that were hastily assembled.

A tasting of the varietal bars was interspersed with the finished confections. Michael meant this to be informal, and passed a few of the gold-wrapped bars to each table, then asked the tasters to break off pieces. When the good-mannered French awkwardly tried to break the bars while still in their wrappers, he realized he should have divided the bars beforehand.

The tasters were reflective while tasting the first two confections, and only one question was asked: "What kind of cardamom do you use?" But the chocolate-covered Key lime pears were so popular that the crowd relaxed a little. The tarragon grapefruit drew more com-

ments: "The grapefruit is a little too acidic for the tarragon." "The grapefruit tastes caramelized." "It's a good marriage." Michael thanked the group for their opinions, and when his words were translated, everyone applauded. The tasting moved to the last confection, the mint tea. Another question, this time in English: "Is it chewing gum mint?" There were some differences of opinion about the intensity of the mint. Some found it too strong; others enjoyed it.

The two *chocolatiers* made the final comments. One pronounced the chocolates "*un bon travail*." The second *chocolatier* said that the chocolates were very good and, with a twinkle in his eye, added, "especially for an American."

Chocolate Barks

Barks are such a simple idea that it is surprising that more confectioners don't make them. Once you have tempered chocolate for dipping centers or filling molds, you can, with a little planning, use the remaining chocolate to make these barks. If you make the toppings ahead, the bark assembly takes only a few minutes. Of course, you can make these luscious treats even if you aren't dipping or molding chocolates by simply tempering chocolate specifically for them. (See instructions for tempering chocolate on page 28.)

Although the toppings differ—some are caramelized nuts, others dried fruits or candied citrus—the basic method is the same. A ⅜-inch-thick layer of tempered chocolate lines a sheet pan and the topping is sprinkled over the surface. Just before the chocolate sets, the bark is cut into pieces.

Store all the barks in an airtight container in a cool, dry place. They will keep for at least 2 weeks.

✢ Cashew-Sesame Dark Chocolate Bark ✢

About 24 pieces

1½ cups (7¼ ounces) whole cashews

½ cup (3½ ounces) granulated cane sugar

2 teaspoons (⅓ ounce) unsalted butter with 82% butterfat

¼ cup (1 ounce) sesame seeds, preferably natural unhulled

½ teaspoon kosher salt

1½ cups (14 ounces by weight) tempered 61% to 70% chocolate

The nuts and seeds are caramelized before they are sprinkled on the tempered chocolate, offering a sweet crunch with each bite.

Roast and caramelize the nuts

- Preheat the oven to 350°F. Line the bottom of a sheet pan with parchment paper.

- Spread the cashews on the prepared pan in a single layer. Roast the nuts until they are a medium brown, about 15 minutes.

- While the nuts are roasting, put a piece of parchment paper or a nonstick baking liner on a work surface. Measure the sugar and butter and put them next to the stove.

- As soon as the nuts are roasted, place a medium heavy-bottomed pot over medium-high heat. Use an unlined copper pot if you have one. When the pot is hot—test by flicking a drop of water into the pan; it should sizzle and dance across the bottom—immediately add the hot nuts and the sugar. Cook, stirring constantly with a wooden spoon, until the sugar liquefies and coats the nuts. If they start to smoke, reduce the heat. When only a few specks of sugar remain unmelted, add the sesame seeds and stir a few times until they are evenly distributed. Remove from the heat, sprinkle the salt over the nuts and seeds, and add the butter. Stir until the nuts glisten and start to separate from one another.

- Scrape the nuts and seeds onto the parchment paper or baking liner and spread them apart. Let the nuts and seeds cool completely, and then break up the larger pieces.

- Store the nuts in a zippered plastic bag at room temperature if you are not making the bark immediately.

Make the bark

- Line the bottom of an 8-by-12-inch sheet pan with parchment paper.

- Pour the tempered chocolate into the prepared pan. Spread it evenly with a small offset spatula. Tap the pan on a work surface to even the top.

- Sprinkle the caramelized nuts and seeds over the chocolate. Tap the pan again to settle the nuts and seeds into the chocolate. When the chocolate loses its sheen and starts to set, after about 15 minutes, cut the bark with a sharp knife into 2-inch squares or other fanciful shapes of your choice. Leave the bark at room temperature until it is completely set, about 15 minutes, and then separate the pieces.

- Store in a cool, dry place, not in the refrigerator.

❧ Dried-Fruit Dark Chocolate Bark ❧

The specific fruits in this recipe are only a suggestion. Substitute your favorites for some or all of them, keeping the amounts and sizes of the fruits the same.

- Mix the dried fruits and crystallized ginger together in a bowl.

- Line the bottom of an 8-by-12-inch sheet pan with parchment paper.

- Pour the tempered chocolate into the prepared pan. Spread it evenly with a small offset spatula. Tap the pan on a work surface to even the top.

- Sprinkle the fruit mixture over the chocolate. Tap the pan again to settle the fruits into the chocolate. When the chocolate loses its sheen and starts to set, after about 15 minutes, cut the bark with a sharp knife into 2-inch squares or other fanciful shapes of your choice. Leave the bark at room temperature until it is completely set, about 1 hour, and then separate the pieces.

- Store in a cool, dry place, not in the refrigerator.

About 24 pieces

½ cup (2 ounces) dried pitted sour cherries

¼ cup (1¼ ounces) dried blueberries

⅓ cup (1¼ ounces) dried cranberries

5 quarter-sized pieces (1¼ ounces) crystallized ginger, chopped into ¼-inch dice

1½ cups (14 ounces by weight) tempered 65% chocolate

✤ Hazelnut, Pumpkin Seed, and Pistachio Dark Chocolate Bark ✤

About 24 pieces

⅓ cup (1½ ounces) whole hazelnuts

¼ cup (1 ounce) shelled pumpkin seeds

⅓ cup (1¾ ounces) shelled green pistachios

1½ cups (14 ounces by weight) tempered 61% to 70% chocolate

½ teaspoon *fleur de sel* in fine grains

The nuts and seeds in this bark aren't caramelized, but they are roasted to bring out their flavor. Make sure they are at room temperature before you sprinkle them on the chocolate.

Roast and caramelize the nuts

- Preheat the oven to 350°F. Line the bottoms of 2 sheet pans with parchment paper.

- Spread the hazelnuts on 1 prepared pan. Mix the pumpkin seeds and pistachios together and spread them on the second prepared pan.

- Roast the hazelnuts until the skins start to darken and shrivel, about 8 minutes. Roast the pumpkin seeds and pistachios until lightly toasted, 8 to 10 minutes.

- Remove the nuts and seeds from the oven. As soon as the hazelnuts are cool enough to handle, rub them in batches in a kitchen towel to remove the skins. Not every bit will come off.

- Roughly chop all of them and mix together in a bowl.

Make the bark

- Line the bottom of an 8-by-12-inch sheet pan with parchment paper.

- Pour the tempered chocolate into the prepared pan. Spread it evenly with a small offset spatula. Tap the pan on a work surface to even the top.

- Sprinkle the roasted nuts and seeds and the *fleur de sel* over the chocolate. Tap the pan again to settle the toppings into the chocolate. When the chocolate loses its sheen and starts to set, after about 15 minutes, cut the bark with a sharp knife into 2-inch squares or other fanciful shapes of your choice. Leave the bark at room temperature until it is completely set, about 1 hour, and then separate the pieces.

- Store in an airtight container in a cool, dry place, not in the refrigerator.

❧ CANDIED ORANGE PEEL EXTRA-BITTER CHOCOLATE BARK ❧

Save the end pieces of candied orange peel for making this bark. The peel should air-dry at room temperature overnight, so begin drying it the day before you plan to make the bark.

Air-dry the candied orange peel

- The day before you make the bark, remove the orange pieces from the syrup and rinse with cool water to remove the syrup. Arrange the pieces on a wire rack placed on a sheet pan. Leave them at room temperature overnight. Roughly chop the pieces. Don't roll the pieces in granulated sugar; the sugar will dissolve in the chocolate.

Make the bark

- Line the bottom of an 8-by-12-inch sheet pan with parchment paper.

- Pour the tempered chocolate into the prepared pan. Spread it evenly with a small offset spatula. Tap the pan on a work surface to even the top.

- Sprinkle the candied orange peel over the chocolate. Tap the pan again to settle the peel into the chocolate. When the chocolate loses its sheen and starts to set, after about 15 minutes, cut the bark with a sharp knife into 2-inch squares or other fanciful shapes of your choice. Leave the bark at room temperature until it is completely set, about 1 hour, and then separate the pieces.

- Store in a cool, dry place, not in the refrigerator.

Variation

- Substitute candied grapefruit peel for the orange peel.

About 24 pieces

1½ cups (8³⁄₄ ounces) candied orange peel (see Candied Citrus Peel, page 114)

1½ cups (14 ounces by weight) tempered 61% to 70% chocolate

❧ Caramelized Peanut Milk Chocolate Bark ❧

About 24 pieces

1½ cups (8 ounces) blanched whole peanuts

½ cup (3½ ounces) granulated cane sugar

2 teaspoons (⅓ ounce) unsalted butter with 82% butterfat

½ teaspoon kosher salt

1 cup (10 ounces by weight) tempered 41% milk chocolate

⅓ cup plus 2 tablespoons (4 ounces by weight) smooth peanut butter, at room temperature

Mixing peanut butter into the chocolate gives this bark an extra dose of peanut taste. Use a smooth peanut butter made from roasted nuts and without added salt or sugar.

If you can't find blanched peanuts, you can blanch them yourself: drop shelled peanuts in boiling water, leave for 1 minute, and then drain the nuts and plunge them in cold water. The skins should slip off easily.

Roast and caramelize the nuts

- Preheat the oven to 350°F. Line the bottom of a sheet pan with parchment paper.

- Spread the peanuts on the prepared pan in a single layer. Roast the nuts until they are a medium brown, about 15 minutes.

- While the nuts are roasting, put a piece of parchment paper or a nonstick baking liner on a work surface. Measure the sugar and butter and put both of them next to the stove.

- As soon as the nuts are roasted, place a medium heavy-bottomed pot over medium-high heat. Use an unlined copper pot if you have one. When the pot is hot—test by flicking a drop of water into the pan; it should sizzle and dance across the bottom—immediately add the hot nuts and the sugar. Cook, stirring constantly with a wooden spoon, until the sugar liquefies and coats the nuts. If they start to smoke, reduce the heat. When only a few specks of sugar remain unmelted, remove from the heat. Sprinkle the salt over the nuts and add the butter. Stir until the nuts glisten and start to separate from one another.

- Scrape the nuts onto the parchment paper or baking liner and spread them apart. Let the nuts cool completely, and then break up the larger pieces. The pieces don't have to be uniform.

- Store the nuts in a zippered plastic bag at room temperature if you are not making the bark immediately.

Make the bark

- Line the bottom of an 8-by-12-inch sheet pan with parchment paper.

- Stir the tempered chocolate and peanut butter together in a medium bowl.

- Pour the chocolate into the prepared pan. Spread it evenly with a small offset spatula. Tap the pan on a work surface to even the top.

- Sprinkle the caramelized nuts over the chocolate. Tap the pan again to settle the nuts into the chocolate. When the chocolate loses its sheen and starts to set, after about 15 minutes, cut the bark with a sharp knife into 2-inch squares or other fanciful shapes of your choice. Leave the bark at room temperature until it is completely set, about 1 hour, and then separate the pieces.

- Store in a cool, dry place, not in the refrigerator.

☙ Caramelized Cocoa Nib White Chocolate Bark ❧

About 24 pieces

1 teaspoon (⅓ ounce) unsalted butter with 82% butterfat

Scant 1½ cups (6 ounces) cocoa nibs

½ cup (3½ ounces) granulated cane sugar

1½ cups (14 ounces by weight) tempered white chocolate

Cocoa nibs, bits of roasted and shelled cocoa beans, have a tannic, smoky flavor with a hint of the chocolate they will become after chocolate makers treat them to a long, slow mixing with cocoa butter and sugar. Caramelizing them softens their rough edges. In this bark, they are a perfect foil for the sweetness of the white chocolate.

Because the caramelized nibs will keep indefinitely, the recipe here makes enough for this bark, the Cocoa Nib Ice Cream on page 170, and the Dried-Fruit Clusters on page 113.

Caramelize the nibs

- Put a piece of parchment paper or a nonstick baking liner on a work surface. Measure the butter and put it next to the stove.

- Put the nibs and sugar in a medium heavy-bottomed pot. Use an unlined copper pot if you have one. Place the pot over high heat and vigorously stir the mixture with a wooden spoon. As the sugar cooks, the mixture will smoke. When only a few specks of sugar remain unmelted, remove from the heat and stir in the butter. The nibs will glisten and separate into small clumps.

- Scrape the nibs onto the parchment paper or baking liner and spread out the individual clumps. Let cool to room temperature and then break into ¼-inch pieces. Store them in a zippered plastic bag at room temperature.

- You will need 1 cup (4 ounces) caramelized nibs for the bark. Reserve the remaining caramelized nibs for other uses.

Make the bark

- Line the bottom of an 8-by-12-inch sheet pan with parchment paper.

- Pour the chocolate into the prepared pan. Spread it evenly with a small offset spatula. Tap the pan on a work surface to even the top.

- Sprinkle the caramelized nibs over the chocolate. When the chocolate loses its sheen and starts to set, after about 15 minutes, cut the bark with a sharp knife into 2-inch squares or other fanciful shapes of your choice. Leave the bark at room temperature until it is completely set, about 1 hour, and then separate the pieces.

- Store in a cool, dry place, not in the refrigerator.

Testing—One, Two, Three

Recchiuti
CONFECTIONS

Producing exquisite fare in a commercial kitchen is one thing. Replicating those same treats at home is another. Doing the math doesn't always work when reducing a recipe for a thousand pieces of ganache to fifty, or hundreds of brownies to sixteen. When we tested the recipes for this book, we constantly juggled ratios of ingredients, striving for the same taste that the larger batches produce. It often took more than one try. The first time we steeped lavender in cream to make ganache it soaked up every drop.

Another variable in the journey from professional to home kitchen is the expertise of the person following the recipe. Repetition enhances skill. Professional confectioners and bakers work quickly and effectively because they make the same recipes again and again. Someone at home, tackling a recipe for the first time, perhaps using unfamiliar ingredients, doesn't have the same advantages.

Acutely aware of these possible pitfalls and wanting this book to be accessible to amateur and expert alike, we sought a cadre of people with varying skills, representative of people likely to use this book, to test the recipes in their home kitchens. We were fortunate to find such a group among the students at San Francisco's Tante Marie's Cooking School, owned by Mary Risley.

They were enrolled in a part-time pastry class that allowed them to work at other jobs. Some were employed in commercial kitchens, while others were in unrelated fields, such as computer programming. All were eager to learn and were as excited to try the recipes as we were to have them: a perfect marriage.

We met at the Recchiuti Confections kitchen one Friday evening and gave everyone recipes; additional instructions, such as how to temper chocolate; and a box of ingredients that included chocolate, invert sugar, vanilla beans, and trans-fer sheets. Some testers were willing to try four recipes, others only two. People who were new to chocolate chose baked items and decided to make truffles instead of dipped or molded chocolates. We sent them off with words of encouragement and planned another meeting two weeks later to taste their efforts and discuss any problems. Then we waited. Were the recipes clear enough? Were the trickier ones too complicated to execute? Would this be a book that worked?

The testers were beaming as we gathered again at the kitchen. Although there were a few glitches, overall the results were impressive. Many of the efforts looked professional. We talked through any problems and made adjustments accordingly in the recipes. The cardamom nougat was too strong; it needed further testing. One brownie recipe, which works beautifully in large batches baked in a commercial convection oven, remained so vapid, even after more testing, that we didn't use it.

The testers' labors were invaluable. They assured us that the recipes did work and made us confident that people who try them will succeed—only an obsession for chocolate is necessary.

CHOCOLATE DRINKS

Chocolate drinks have come a long way from the concoctions made by the Aztecs and the Mayans. Those early libations lacked the smooth chocolate we have today, and their harshness wasn't tempered with sugar.

The offerings in this chapter add panache to the humble childhood drink. They're made with finished chocolate instead of cocoa powder, are carefully matched with spices and other flavors, and are often given an extra jolt with a few tablespoons of chocolate sauce or caramel base. If you wish, float marshmallows on top or sprinkle them with cocoa powder or cinnamon.

For the best results, grate the chocolate on the largest holes of a box grater-shredder and use an immersion blender to whip the ingredients together.

⊂ಾ Dark Chocolate Mint Drink ಾ⊃

2 servings

1 ¾ cups (14 ounces) whole milk

2 tablespoons packed julienned fresh peppermint leaves

2 ounces 61% to 65% chocolate, grated

2 Tahitian Vanilla Bean Marshmallows (page 97)

Mint's intensity matches the flavor of the dark chocolate in this drink. This version is made with peppermint, but use a different mint, such as spearmint, if you prefer.

- Bring the milk to a boil in a small saucepan over medium heat. Remove from the heat and whisk in the mint leaves. Cover the top of the pan with plastic wrap and let steep for 15 minutes.

- After 15 minutes, remove the plastic wrap and bring the milk back to a simmer. Pour it into a 1-quart clear vessel. Add the chocolate.

- Blend with an immersion blender until the chocolate has melted and the drink is smooth.

- Put a marshmallow in each cup. Holding a fine-mesh sieve over each cup (to strain out the mint), pour the drink over the marshmallow, and then serve.

⚭ Dark Varietal Chocolate Drink ⚭

The chocolates made from a single variety of cocoa bean highlight the bean's individual flavors: the berry and spice of the Colombian, the earthy intensity of the Ecuadorian, or the deep fruity tones of the Venezuelan. Taste the chocolates and decide which one to use for this drink, or make the same recipe with different varietals and compare.

Use this same recipe to make drinks from 70% chocolate, or if you like a bold, strong chocolate taste, use an 80% chocolate.

- Bring the milk to a simmer in a small saucepan over medium heat. Pour it into a 1-quart clear vessel. Add the chocolate sauce and the grated chocolate.

- Blend with an immersion blender until the chocolate has melted and the drink is smooth.

- Pour into cups and serve.

2 servings

1½ cups (12 ounces) whole milk

2 tablespoons (1¼ ounces) Extra-Bitter Chocolate Sauce (page 159)

2 ounces single-bean varietal chocolate, grated

❧ Milk Chocolate with Burnt Caramel Drink ❧

2 servings

1½ cups (12 ounces) whole milk

3 tablespoons (2 ounces by weight) Burnt Caramel Base (page 70), at room temperature

2 ounces 41% milk chocolate, grated

The burnt caramel adds a welcome complexity to this drink by tempering the milky, slightly sweet tones of the chocolate.

- Bring the milk to a simmer in a small saucepan over medium heat. Pour the hot milk into a 1-quart clear vessel. Add the burnt caramel and the grated chocolate.

- Blend with an immersion blender until the chocolate has melted and the drink is smooth.

- Pour into cups and serve.

BURNT CARAMEL, ONE OF
MICHAEL'S FAVORITE TASTES

Who would want to eat burnt anything? The notion evokes blackened, shriveled morsels seared into inedibility. Usually recipes caution about cooking a caramel sauce too long. It will taste bitter and burnt, they admonish. Paradoxically, Michael knows that this is the way to get the most out of sugar. He learned this trick from candy makers of the old school in Boston during one of his many apprenticeships. Because the burnt caramel isn't used alone, but is truly a base, it needs to be as intense as possible. If the sugar is cooked only until it turns a light amber, the addition of an ice-cream custard, some cream to make a sauce, or a highly flavorful chocolate will diminish its potency.

So making this base is almost foolproof. Let it burn. That's what you want.

A majestic copper cauldron at Recchiuti Confections stands in one corner of the room. An electric lift lowers the kettle to the heat source—coils of wire that glow red. Although it is used for many purposes, the confectioners affectionately call it the caramel cooker. It lives up to its name during the marathon sessions when Michael and his crew make massive quantities of caramel sauce for a wholesale customer. Because the sugar smokes as it blackens and then hisses steam when water is added to arrest the cooking, the air in the workroom doesn't have a chance to clear between batches. But the hearty confectioners press on, burning sugar until the order is filled.

∽ Milk Chocolate Chai ∽

2 servings

3 tablespoons chai tea

1 cup (8 ounces) water

1 cup (8 ounces) whole milk

2 ounces 41% milk chocolate, grated

Use your favorite chai tea to make this drink. Michael likes a tea spiced with cinnamon, ginger, cardamom, cloves, and pepper.

- Put the tea in a small heatproof bowl. Bring the water to a boil in a small saucepan and pour it over the tea. Steep the tea for 5 minutes, stirring occasionally. Strain the tea through a sieve lined with cheesecloth, pushing down on the leaves with the back of a spoon. Pour the tea into a 1-quart clear vessel.

- Bring the milk to a simmer in a small saucepan over medium heat. Add the hot milk to the tea, and then add the grated chocolate.

- Blend with an immersion blender until the chocolate has melted and the drink is smooth.

- Pour into cups, leaving any sediment in the bottom of the vessel, and serve.

⌒ Milk Chocolate Malt Drink ⌒

William Horlick, an English American, manufactured the first malted milk—and thus the first dried whole milk with a shelf life—in 1883, in Wisconsin. In England, malt was considered nutritious due to its sugar, B vitamins, and mineral content, and was added to various foods, including cocoa drinks. Even the original *Joy of Cooking* lists malt as an ingredient for a chocolate drink to give it extra food value. Possible nutritional worth aside, this is a drink with an old-fashioned flavor.

- Put the cream and milk in a small saucepan. Scrape the vanilla seeds from the bean into the pan and then add the bean. Bring to a simmer over medium heat.

- Strain the milk through a sieve into a clear 1-quart vessel. Add the malt syrup and the chocolate.

- Blend with an immersion blender until the chocolate has melted and the drink is smooth.

- Pour into cups and serve.

2 servings

¼ cup (2 ounces) heavy whipping cream

1½ cups (12 ounces) whole milk

½ Tahitian vanilla bean, split horizontally

3 tablespoons (2¼ ounces by weight) unhopped barley-malt syrup

2 ounces 41% milk chocolate, grated

⤫ White Chocolate Mocha Drink ⤫

2 servings

1½ cups (12 ounces) whole milk

1 Tahitian vanilla bean, split horizontally

3 ounces white chocolate, grated

2 tablespoons (1 ounce) hot brewed espresso or double-strength coffee

Because white chocolate lacks cocoa liquor, the essence of chocolate, it is mildly flavored and sweeter than dark chocolate. The coffee adds some acidity and roasted notes that counter the chocolate's sweetness.

If you have an espresso machine, use it to make the coffee. Otherwise, make a small amount of double-strength coffee.

- Put the milk in a small saucepan. Scrape the vanilla seeds from the bean into the pan. Bring to a simmer over medium heat. Pour the hot milk into a 1-quart clear vessel. Add the grated chocolate.

- Blend with an immersion blender until the chocolate has melted and the drink is smooth.

- Pour into cups. Stir 1 tablespoon coffee into each cup and serve.

Sauces

Warm chocolate sauce inching down a dish of ice cream, its heat softening the rich, creamy scoops as the cold sets it, is a picture of comforting childhood times. You will evoke such memories and delight both children and adults with the sauces that follow.

In addition to using these sauces for making sundaes, you can drizzle a chocolate or caramel sauce over a wedge of cake or a plate of crepes or waffles. You can also put a bowl of your favorite chocolate sauce alongside a platter of sliced apples or pears or whole strawberries and let guests make their own chocolate-cloaked morsels for dessert. And in a chocolate emergency, you can even eat the sauce straight from the jar.

— Burnt Caramel Sauce —

About 3 cups

2 cups (14 ounces) granulated
cane sugar

1 cup plus 2 tablespoons (9 ounces)
heavy whipping cream

½ cup (5⅓ ounces by weight) light
corn syrup

10 tablespoons (5 ounces) unsalted
butter with 82% butterfat, at room
temperature

Here's another use for Michael's favorite flavor. The caramelized sugar smokes and sputters when the cream is added, so turn on the exhaust fan in your kitchen when making this sauce. Be very careful, too, as the sugar is extremely hot.

Corn syrup is often added to sugar before cooking to prevent crystallization, but in this instance, it is added later, which speeds up caramelization.

- Put the sugar in a medium heavy-bottomed pot. Use an unlined copper pot if you have one. Place over medium heat and cook, stirring occasionally with a wooden spoon, until the sugar melts. Then continue to cook, without stirring, until the sugar turns black, about 10 minutes. If any crystals form on the sides of the pan as the sugar darkens, wash them down with a wet pastry brush. Just before it turns black, the sugar syrup may foam up. If it does, reduce the heat to low and, wearing an oven mitt, carefully stir it down. When the sugar syrup is ready, it will smoke and large bubbles will break on the surface.

- While the sugar is cooking, bring the cream to a boil in a small saucepan over medium heat. When the sugar is black, remove the pot from the heat and carefully stir in the corn syrup. Put a sieve or splatter guard over the pot. Wearing an oven mitt, slowly pour the hot cream into the sugar syrup a little at a time. The mixture will sputter and foam. Be careful, as it is very hot. Whisk in the butter.

- Pour the finished sauce into a bowl and let cool for about 5 minutes before using. If not using immediately, let it cool to room temperature, pour into a jar, cover, and refrigerate. It will keep for at least 1 month. It may separate under storage; simply stir it to recombine. To reheat, stir over low heat.

~ Dark Chocolate Orange Sauce ~

Orange and chocolate top nearly everyone's chart of favorite flavor marriages, which is what makes this sauce so appealing. If you have candied orange peel on hand, chop some and pair it with the sauce for an extra dose of orange. Use a Microplane grater to zest the orange.

About 2½ cups

9 ounces 70% chocolate, coarsely chopped

1½ cups (12 ounces) heavy whipping cream

1 orange

2 cups (16 ounces) fresh orange juice (6 to 8 large oranges)

¼ cup (1¾ ounces) granulated cane sugar

1 Tahitian vanilla bean, split horizontally

- Put the chocolate in a medium stainless-steel bowl.

- Pour the cream into a small saucepan. Finely grate the zest from the orange directly into the pan. (The orange can then be juiced as part of the 2 cups fresh orange juice.) Place over medium heat and bring to a boil. Remove from the heat and cover the top of the pan with plastic wrap. Let steep for 30 minutes.

- While the cream is steeping, reduce the orange juice: Put the juice into a small saucepan and stir in the sugar. Scrape the vanilla seeds from the bean into the pan and then add the bean. Bring to a moderate boil over medium-high heat and cook, stirring occasionally with a rubber spatula, until the juice reduces by half (1 cup/8 ounces), about 15 minutes. Remove from the heat.

- After the cream has steeped for 30 minutes, remove the plastic and bring the cream to a simmer over medium heat. Add the reduced orange juice, bring to a boil, and remove from the heat.

- Strain through a fine-mesh sieve directly into the chocolate. Whisk until the chocolate is melted.

- Pour the sauce into a 1-quart clear vessel. Blend with an immersion blender until smooth.

- Either use immediately, or let cool to room temperature, pour into a jar, cover, and refrigerate. It will keep for at least 1 month. To reheat, stir over low heat.

~ Dark Chocolate Malt Sauce ~

About 3 cups

¾ cup (3 ounces) unsweetened natural cocoa powder

⅔ cup (8 ounces by weight) unhopped barley-malt syrup

1¾ cups (14 ounces) heavy whipping cream

1 cup (7 ounces) granulated cane sugar

6 ounces 65% chocolate, coarsely chopped

¼ teaspoon kosher salt

Malt is a distinctive flavor that goes surprisingly well with chocolate, especially in this sauce where it seems to make the chocolate more pronounced. This would be perfect over Vanilla Bean Ice Cream or drizzled on spice cake.

- Sift the cocoa powder into a small bowl.

- Put the malt syrup, cream, and sugar in a medium heavy-bottomed saucepan. Whisk to combine. Place over medium heat and bring to a simmer. Whisk in the cocoa powder. Bring to a boil while whisking constantly, then boil for 1 minute while whisking occasionally.

- Remove from the heat and add the chocolate and salt. Whisk until the chocolate is melted.

- Pour the sauce into a 1-quart clear vessel. Blend with an immersion blender until smooth.

- Either use immediately, or let cool to room temperature, pour into a jar, cover, and refrigerate. It will keep for at least 1 month. To reheat, stir over low heat.

~ Milk Chocolate Sauce ~

About 3 cups

¼ cup (2⅔ ounces by weight) light corn syrup

1½ cups (12 ounces) heavy whipping cream

1 Tahitian vanilla bean, split horizontally

8 ounces 41% milk chocolate, coarsely chopped

3 ounces white chocolate, coarsely chopped

¼ teaspoon kosher salt

The new milk chocolates, with their high percentage of cocoa mass, have a fuller chocolate taste than old-style milk chocolates. The more intense chocolate taste provides a better balance with the sugar, resulting in a sauce that isn't overly sweet.

- Put the corn syrup and cream into a medium saucepan. Scrape the seeds from the vanilla bean into the pan. Place over medium heat and bring to a boil.

- Remove from the heat and add both chocolates and the salt. Whisk until the chocolate is melted.

- Pour the sauce into a 1-quart clear vessel. Blend with an immersion blender until smooth.

- Either use immediately, or let cool to room temperature, pour it into a jar, cover, and refrigerate. It will keep for at least 2 weeks. To reheat, stir over low heat.

‒ Extra-Bitter Chocolate Sauce ‒

A hefty dose of unsweetened natural cocoa powder is the base for this sauce. It is dark and thick and possesses an essence of chocolate taste. Natural cocoa powder, although lighter in color than Dutch-processed cocoa, has a truer chocolate flavor.

- Sift the cocoa powder into a small bowl.

- Put the sugar, cream, corn syrup, water, vanilla extract, and salt in a medium heavy-bottomed saucepan. Scrape the seeds from the vanilla bean into the pan. Place over medium heat and whisk until all the ingredients are blended. Add the cocoa powder. Reduce the heat to low and whisk constantly. The sauce will get lumpy, but then become smooth as it cooks. Cook until it just begins to boil. This should take about 8 minutes. Be careful that it does not burn.

- Pour the sauce into a 1-quart clear vessel. Blend with an immersion blender until smooth.

- Either use immediately, or pour the finished sauce into a bowl, let cool to room temperature, pour into a jar, cover, and refrigerate. It will keep for at least 1 month. To reheat, stir over low heat.

About 3 cups

1¼ cups (5 ounces) unsweetened natural cocoa powder

1⅓ cups (9½ ounces) granulated cane sugar

1½ cups (12 ounces) heavy whipping cream

⅓ cup (3½ ounces by weight) light corn syrup

2 tablespoons water

2 tablespoons pure vanilla extract, preferably Madagascar Bourbon

¼ teaspoon kosher salt

½ Madagascar Bourbon vanilla bean, split horizontally

– Raspberry White Chocolate Sauce with Thyme –

About 2½ cups

3 pints (16 ounces) raspberries

3 tablespoons (1½ ounces) granulated cane sugar

1½ cups (12 ounces) heavy whipping cream

2 teaspoons fresh thyme leaves

9 ounces white chocolate, coarsely chopped

2 tablespoons (1 ounce) butter with 82% butterfat, very soft (75°F)

Here, the acidity of the berries tames the sweetness of the white chocolate. This is a sauce to spoon over perfectly ripe summer fruit or drizzle over a fruit pie or tart. Unlike the other sauces, all of which taste best when warm or hot, this one should be served at room temperature if it is accompanying fruit.

- Purée the raspberries in a food processor, then push them through a fine-mesh sieve to remove the seeds. You should have 1 cup (8 ounces).

- Put the berry purée in a small saucepan and stir in the sugar. Place over medium heat, bring to a simmer, and cook, stirring occasionally with a rubber spatula, until the purée reduces by half (½ cup/4 ounces), about 15 minutes.

- Put the cream and thyme in a small saucepan. Place over medium heat, bring to a boil, and remove from the heat.

- Add the raspberry purée and the chocolate to the hot cream. Whisk until the chocolate is melted.

- Pour the sauce into a 1-quart clear vessel. Blend with an immersion blender until smooth. Add the butter and again blend until smooth. Strain the sauce through the fine-mesh sieve to remove the thyme leaves.

- Use immediately or let cool to room temperature before using. Or, pour the sauce into a jar, cover, and refrigerate. It will keep for at least 2 weeks. Bring to room temperature before serving or stir over low heat to reheat.

A Quest for the Best

We wanted to see the lavender fields and time was short. The farmers planned to harvest the intensely aromatic flowers atop their thin square stems within a week. Then the flowers would be gone, leaving mounds of green-gray foliage that wouldn't bloom again for another year.

Michael buys the dried flowers and fresh lemon verbena, both of which he uses to infuse cream for ganaches, from Eatwell Farm. His lemon verbena supply was depleted, and he hoped to replenish it on this visit. "The car will smell like lemon verbena on the way home," he said.

And so the adventure began. Because Maren, the photographer for this book, joined us, we strove for a predawn arrival to capture the best light. San Francisco was dark and couched in a light fog as we drove through the quiet streets and onto the Bay Bridge, heading east. The light traffic held, and we reached the bridge over the Carquinez Strait at the top of San Francisco Bay shortly after four-thirty. Michael steered to the carpool lane and was perplexed when the attendant asked for the toll. We were too early—carpools aren't honored until five.

After forty more minutes, we turned off the freeway at the small town of Dixon, still in the dark. An earthy aroma permeated the car, signaling that we were in farmland. After a few more turns, "Eatwell" scrawled on a piece of wood by the side of the road announced our destination. We crossed a culvert over an irrigation ditch, passed a gurgling water pump, and parked near the edge of a large field. A few tractors, pickup trucks, shipping containers, and hooped enclosures greeted us. The workers had not yet arrived.

Light from a full moon barely illuminated the plants. We could make out waves of varying hues of purple arranged in rows. Maren set up her tripod and Michael and I wandered into the fields. The ground between the rows was parched and cracked;

Recchiuti
CONFECTIONS

when the plants are in bloom, less water means more scent, so these plants were no longer irrigated.

Three stacks of beehives, twelve to a stack, stood at the entrance to the field. A beekeper leaves them here not to pollinate the lavender—wild bumblebees do that—but to make lavender honey. In the heat of the day, their numbers hum in the fields as they collect nectar and pollen, but in the chilly hours of predawn, they were huddled inside.

When the sky began to lighten, the workers arrived in twos and threes, climbing out of various vehicles. A quick meeting was conducted in Spanish, and then some of the people drove off to another part of the farm. The remaining three men and six women made up the lavender harvest crew.

I thought that one of the tractors would be employed, but the crew walked right past it, armed only with one pair of long-handled loppers. They stopped at the end of the first row of plants whose flowers were intensely purple. Two of the men encircled bunches of lavender in their hands, about halfway up the stems. With two whacks of the loppers the third man cut each bunch close to the junction where the stems met the plant. The women followed, slipping rubber

bands over the stems of each bunch, and then piling the bunches on the cropped plants. As the bunches collected, another woman cradled as many as she could carry in her arms and walked them to a hooped enclosure where they would be hung for drying. To call this hands-on operation a harvest overamplifies it. Cutting is a better description.

Eatwell grows several varieties of lavender. The first planting in 1994, a modest thirty-five plants, now numbers in the thousands and spans six acres. That morning, the workers cut the variety 'Grosso' with flowers still closed, ideal for drying. After the flowers open, they are distilled into essential oil at a distiller–cabinet maker's facility a valley away to the west. The farm sells other varieties in bouquets at their booth at the Ferry Plaza Farmers' Market in San Francisco.

Michael asked about the lemon verbena. The small shrubs were barely visible; tall weeds surrounded each plant. Because Eatwell farms its crops organically, workers hoe the weeds by hand. But there was lavender to cut, so the lemon verbena would have to wait. And so would Michael.

ICE CREAMS

Only one of these recipes has a chocolate base, but others rely on Michael's infusion technique and his signature flavor. The vanilla ice cream, which has a pureness of its own, provides you with a perfect excuse to accompany it with one of the chocolate sauces. For a dressed-up version of a childhood treat, buy waffle cones, dip the tops in tempered chocolate, and then slip in a scoop of any of these ice creams.

Most commercial ice creams contain stabilizers and artificial flavors, as well as a hefty amount of air. Although many high-end brands are tasty, none are as good as an ice cream that you churn yourself. Home churning lets you use the best ingredients and pure flavors, and the slower speed of home machines does not incorporate much air.

All these recipes were tested in machines that have an insert that is chilled in the freezer before making the ice cream. Other home models, either electric or cooled by ice, can be used with success.

Most of the liquid bases for these ice creams are steeped with flavorings to extract every drop of flavor, some for only a half hour, others overnight. All of the bases are chilled overnight before churning, so although the active preparation time is short, the elapsed time can be up two days. Then, with just a short churning, you have a luscious frozen treat.

If you prefer very soft ice cream, serve these directly from the churn. If your taste is for firmer ice cream that slowly melts in your mouth, transfer it from the churn into another container and freeze it until it becomes harder. All of them, however, are best when eaten within two weeks.

❦ BURNT CARAMEL ICE CREAM ❦

1 quart

1²/₃ cups (13 ounces) whole milk

¾ cup (5¼ ounces) granulated cane sugar, divided

½ Tahitian vanilla bean, split horizontally

6 (4½ ounces) extra-large egg yolks

¾ cup (6 ounces) heavy whipping cream

½ cup (5¼ ounces by weight) Burnt Caramel Base (page 70), chilled

Burnt caramel, Michael's signature flavor, lends its intensity to this remarkable ice cream. Serve it unaccompanied to showcase its flavor.

Because of the sweetness of the caramel base, this ice cream is softer after churning than other ice creams.

- Stir the milk and ½ cup (3½ ounces) of the sugar together in a saucepan. Scrape the vanilla seeds from the bean into the pan and then add the bean. Bring the milk to a boil over medium heat. Remove from the heat, cover the top of the pan with plastic wrap, and let steep for 1 hour.
- Strain the milk through a sieve and return to the saucepan. Bring to a simmer over medium heat.
- While the milk is reheating, combine the egg yolks and the remaining ¼ cup (1³/₄ ounces) sugar in the bowl of a stand mixer fitted with the whip attachment. Beat on medium-high speed until the mixture is pale and thick and forms a ribbon when the whip is lifted from the bowl, 3 to 5 minutes.
- Switch the mixer to low speed. Slowly pour the hot milk into the bowl and beat just until combined. Do not beat to a froth.
- Return the mixture to the saucepan and cook over medium heat, stirring constantly, until the custard coats a spoon and registers 160°F on an instant-read thermometer, about 5 minutes.
- Pour through a sieve into a bowl. Stir in the cream and the Burnt Caramel Base. Cover the bowl and refrigerate the custard overnight.
- The next day, churn the custard in an ice-cream maker according to the manufacturer's instructions.

COLOMBIAN CHOCOLATE MALT ICE CREAM

Because there are no eggs in this ice cream, the texture is lighter than those made with custards. But the taste is unmistakably chocolate, with a hint of malt flavor.

- Put the chocolate in a stainless-steel bowl.

- Stir the milk, cream, and sugar together in a medium saucepan. Bring to a boil over medium heat. Remove from the heat and stir in the malt syrup. Pour the hot liquid over the chocolate and let sit for 5 minutes.

- Whisk the mixture to combine the chocolate with the liquid. Then blend with an immersion blender until the liquid is smooth and no chocolate particles are visible.

- Pour the ice-cream base into a smaller bowl, cover the bowl, and refrigerate overnight.

- The next day, churn the base in an ice-cream maker according to the manufacturer's instructions.

1 quart

5½ ounces 65% Colombian chocolate, coarsely chopped

1¾ cups (14 ounces) whole milk

¾ cup (6 ounces) heavy whipping cream

½ cup (3½ ounces) granulated cane sugar

2½ teaspoons unhopped barley-malt syrup

❧ Meyer Lemon–Buttermilk Ice Cream ❧

1 quart

³/₄ cup (6 ounces) heavy whipping cream

²/₃ cup (4²/₃ ounces) granulated cane sugar, divided into halves

1 Meyer lemon

½ Tahitian vanilla bean, split horizontally

⅓ cup (3 ounces) whole milk

6 (4½ ounces) extra-large egg yolks

1¼ cups (10 ounces) buttermilk, chilled

3 tablespoons (1½ ounces) fresh Meyer lemon juice (about 2 lemons)

The Meyer lemon, a hybrid with a lemon and a mandarin orange for parents, was introduced into California by the botanist Frank Meyer in 1914. It quickly became a backyard tree, prized for its fruit and ornamental value. If you live in a citrus-friendly climate, consider planting a tree for an ample supply of these special fruits.

Because the acidity of the lemon zest might curdle milk while it infuses, only cream is used for the infusion. The cream steeps overnight before making the custard, which also chills overnight, so you will need to start making the ice cream at least 2 days before serving.

- Stir the cream and ⅓ cup (2½ ounces) of the sugar together in a small saucepan. Finely grate the zest from the lemon directly into the pan. (The lemon can then be juiced as part of the 3 tablespoons fresh lemon juice.) Scrape the vanilla seeds from the bean into the pan and then add the bean. Bring the cream to a boil over medium heat. Turn off the heat, cover the top of the pan with plastic wrap, and let cool to room temperature. Transfer to a bowl, cover, and refrigerate overnight.

- The next day, strain the cream through a fine-mesh sieve and return to the saucepan. Add the milk. Bring to a simmer over medium heat.

- While the cream mixture is heating, combine the egg yolks and the remaining ⅓ cup (2½ ounces) sugar in the bowl of a stand mixer fitted with the whip attachment. Beat on medium-high speed until the mixture is pale and thick and forms a ribbon when the whip is lifted from the bowl, 3 to 5 minutes.

- Switch the mixer to low speed. Slowly pour the hot cream mixture into the bowl and beat just until combined. Do not beat to a froth.

- Return the mixture to the saucepan and cook over medium heat, stirring constantly, until the custard coats a spoon and registers 160°F on an instant-read thermometer, about 5 minutes.

- Pour through the fine-mesh sieve into a bowl. Cover the bowl and refrigerate the custard overnight.

- The next day, add the buttermilk and lemon juice to the custard and stir to mix. Churn the custard in an ice-cream maker according to the manufacturer's instructions.

❧ Roasted Banana Ice Cream ❧

This is a banana lover's treat. Roasting the fruit intensifies its flavor, and the cream-rich custard smoothes its texture. For a double dose of chocolate, add some brownie bits and top with a generous spoonful of Extra-Bitter Chocolate Sauce (page 159).

- Preheat the oven to 400°F.

- Put the banana, still in its skin, in a small baking dish. Roast until the skin is black and is starting to bubble, about 25 minutes. Let the banana cool completely, and then peel it and mash with a fork. Cover and refrigerate until needed.

- Stir the milk and ⅓ cup (2½ ounces) of the sugar together in a small saucepan. Scrape the vanilla seeds from the bean into the pan and then add the bean. Bring the milk to a boil over medium heat. Remove from the heat, cover the top of the pan with plastic wrap, and let steep for 1 hour.

- Strain the milk through a fine-mesh sieve and return to the saucepan. Bring to a simmer over medium heat.

- While the milk is reheating, combine the egg yolks and the remaining ⅓ cup (2½ ounces) sugar in the bowl of a stand mixer fitted with the whip attachment. Beat on medium-high speed until the mixture is pale and thick and forms a ribbon when the whip is lifted from the bowl, 3 to 5 minutes.

- Switch the mixer to low speed. Slowly pour the hot milk mixture into the bowl and beat just until combined. Do not beat to a froth.

- Return the mixture to the saucepan and cook over medium heat, stirring constantly, until the custard coats a spoon and registers 160°F on an instant-read thermometer, about 5 minutes.

- Pour through the fine-mesh sieve into a bowl and stir in the cream. Cover the bowl and refrigerate the custard overnight.

- The next day, churn the custard in an ice-cream maker according to the manufacturer's instructions. Fold the banana and the brownie bits into the ice cream by hand.

1 quart

1 ripe, medium banana with deep yellow skin

1¼ cups (10 ounces) whole milk

⅔ cup (4⅔ ounces) granulated cane sugar, divided into halves

½ Tahitian vanilla bean, split horizontally

4 (3 ounces) extra-large egg yolks

2 cups (16 ounces) heavy whipping cream

2 brownies, each 2 inches square, cut into ¼-inch pieces (see Rocky Recchiuti Brownies, page 101, or Fudge Brownies, page 99)

❧ Cocoa Nib Ice Cream with Caramelized Cocoa Nibs ❧

1 quart

1²⁄₃ cups (13 ounces) whole milk

½ cup plus ⅓ cup (6 ounces) granulated cane sugar, divided

¼ cup plus 3 tablespoons (1¾ ounces) cocoa nibs

½ Tahitian vanilla bean, split horizontally

5 (3¾ ounces) extra-large egg yolks

¾ cup plus 2 tablespoons (7 ounces) heavy whipping cream

¾ cup (3 ounces) caramelized cocoa nibs (see Caramelized Cocoa Nib White Chocolate Bark, page 140)

This ice cream, flavored with cocoa nibs and vanilla that are steeped in the milk that goes into the custard base, can certainly stand on its own. But folding caramelized cocoa nibs into the freshly churned ice cream raises it to greater heights.

- Stir the milk, ½ cup (3½ ounces) of the sugar, and the cocoa nibs together in a small saucepan. Scrape the vanilla seeds from the bean into the pan and then add the bean. Bring the milk to a boil over medium heat. Remove from the heat, cover the top of the pan with plastic wrap, and let steep for 30 minutes.

- Strain the milk through a fine-mesh sieve and return to the saucepan. Bring to a simmer over medium heat.

- While the milk is reheating, combine the egg yolks and the remaining ⅓ cup (2½ ounces) sugar in the bowl of a stand mixer fitted with the whip attachment. Beat on medium-high speed until the mixture is pale and thick and forms a ribbon when the whip is lifted from the bowl, 3 to 5 minutes.

- Switch the mixer to low speed. Slowly pour the hot milk mixture into the bowl and beat just until combined. Do not beat to a froth.

- Return the mixture to the saucepan and cook over medium heat, stirring constantly, until the custard coats a spoon and registers 160°F on an instant-read thermometer, about 5 minutes.

- Pour through the fine-mesh sieve into a bowl and stir in the cream. Cover the bowl and refrigerate the custard overnight.

- The next day, churn the custard in an ice-cream maker according to the manufacturer's instructions. Fold the caramelized cocoa nibs into the ice cream by hand.

❧ Vanilla Bean Ice Cream ☙

1 quart

1¼ cups (10 ounces) whole milk

⅔ cup (4⅔ ounces) granulated cane sugar, divided into halves

½ Tahitian vanilla bean, split horizontally

6 (4½ ounces) extra-large egg yolks

1½ cups (12 ounces) heavy whipping cream

This is real vanilla ice cream, flavored by the seeds of floral Tahitian beans, not by extract. The seeds are small enough to pass through the sieve and are dispersed throughout the ice cream, heralding its authenticity.

Although it means starting to make the ice cream 2 days ahead of serving, steeping the vanilla in the milk overnight intensifies the final flavor.

- Stir the milk and ⅓ cup (2⅓ ounces) of the sugar together in a small saucepan. Scrape the vanilla seeds from the bean into the pan and then add the bean. Bring the milk to a boil over medium heat. Remove from the heat, cover the top of the pan with plastic wrap, and let steep for at least 1 hour at room temperature, or preferably overnight in the refrigerator.

- Strain the milk through a fine-mesh sieve and return to the saucepan. Bring to a simmer over medium heat.

- While the milk is reheating, combine the egg yolks and the remaining ⅓ cup (2⅓ ounces) sugar in the bowl of a stand mixer fitted with the whip attachment. Beat on medium-high speed until the mixture is pale and thick and forms a ribbon when the whip is lifted from the bowl, 3 to 5 minutes.

- Switch the mixer to low speed. Slowly pour the hot milk mixture into the bowl and beat just until combined. Do not beat to a froth.

- Return the mixture to the saucepan and cook over medium heat, stirring constantly, until the custard coats a spoon and registers 160°F on an instant-read thermometer, about 5 minutes.

- Pour through the fine-mesh sieve into a bowl and stir in the cream. Cover the bowl and refrigerate the custard overnight.

- The next day, churn the custard in an ice-cream maker according to the manufacturer's instructions.

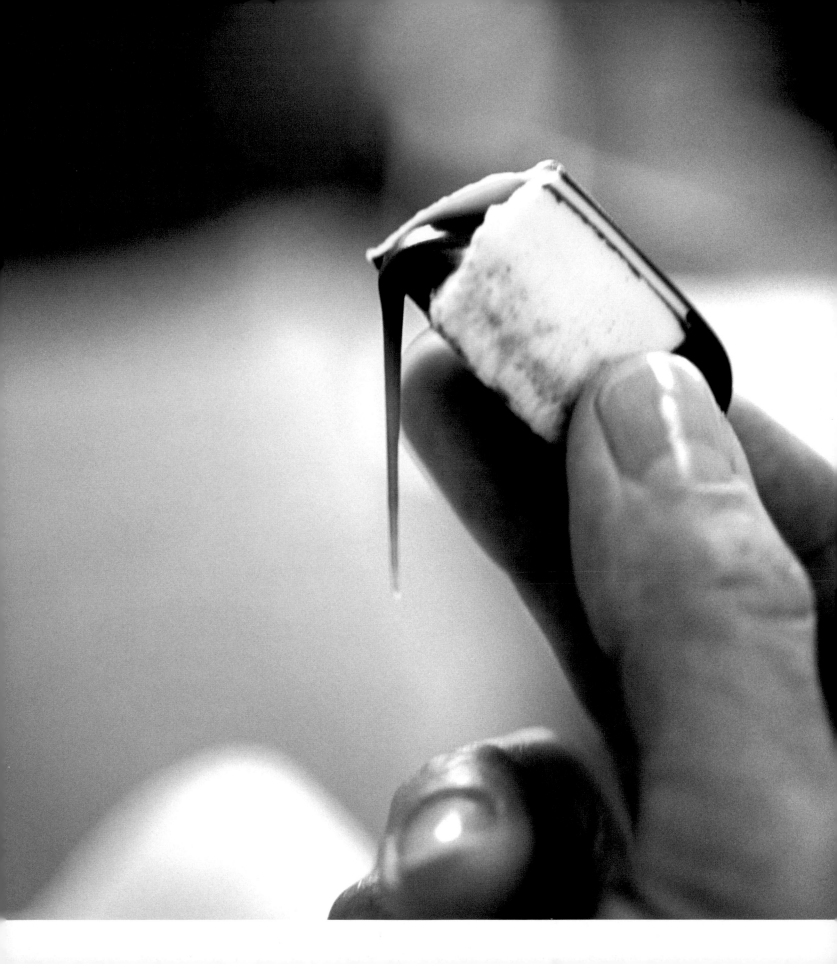

A CHOCOLATE
TASTING PARTY

A Chocolate-Tasting Party

You can show off your chocolate-making savvy and share the taste of great chocolate with your friends by having a chocolate party. It's easier than hosting a dinner, which is typically fraught with last-minute preparations. And the timing is flexible—an afternoon party works just as well as an evening get-together. Make the chocolates leisurely over a span of one or two weeks, choosing a variety of contrasting tastes and shapes, such as molded chocolates and rolled truffles, asymmetrical pieces of barks and classy caramels. You don't have to limit the menu to confections. Cupcakes, cookies, marshmallows, and miniature brownies would also be welcome. Make some recipes that require relatively little work and try others that are more challenging. Then, on the big day, set a table with platters of your beautiful creations. Guests can mingle, tasting and talking, and the best part is that you can join them because you have done all the work ahead.

Chocolate drinks, along with mineral water, are one option for beverages, but what else pairs well with chocolate? Many food and wine writers have addressed the possibilities, and they don't always agree, so we decided to stage a chocolate and beverage tasting to see what works. The group was divided between wine people and confection people. From the first invitational phone call, the wine group offered unsolicited opinions: "Red wine and chocolate is just stupid." "Cabernet with chocolate is the kiss of death." A few volunteered to bring beverages they deemed appropriate. In contrast, only one confection person, an Alsatian, brought a selection of eaux-de-vie and Armagnac.

"Cabernet with chocolate is the kiss of death."

We met at eleven o'clock on a sunny August morning in San Francisco. In front of each participant sat a plate of eight confections, selected because they offered diverse flavors. A phalanx of glasses stood behind each plate. Bottles of possibilities covered the center of the table. A dry California Gewürztraminer; two late-harvest white wines, one a California Viognier and the other a Côteaux du Layon; a Chenin Blanc from the Loire Valley; a fruity Californian Zinfandel, and an Australian Cabernet Sauvignon anchored one end of the table. An aged rum, the Armagnac, a single-malt whiskey, and a dark porter beer occupied the other. The eaux-de-vie stayed iced in the freezer. The balance of the selection was made up of fortified wines, including a sweet Marsala; two Madeiras, both of them Malmsey and aged in wood, one five years old and one ten years old; an East India cream sherry; a ruby port; and a Banyuls.

After Michael explained the composition of each chocolate, we thought about how to proceed. Starting with the stronger chocolates was the obvious choice, but that meant that the stronger beverages would also be first, and it was still before noon. Nonetheless we forged ahead, and after a few rounds, some of the beverages, including the eaux-de-vie that stayed in the freezer, obviously weren't a good match, no matter which chocolate was being tasted. The Zinfandel, bursting with ripe fruit when sipped alone, lost that charm when paired with any of the chocolates and tasted acidic, as did the Cabernet. The spirits seemed overwhelmingly harsh, their high alcohol stripping the chocolate of flavor. And the porter's bitterness clashed with the chocolate's complexities. The late-harvest white wines, including the one brought by a wine-merchant taster as an example of what didn't go with chocolate, paired well with some but not all of the selections.

As the tasting continued, the group gravitated toward the fortified wines in the middle of the table. Two pairings were unanimous: we chose Marsala as the best match with the tarragon-grapefruit confection, and the cream sherry complemented the hazelnut ganache–filled chocolate. A close second with the hazelnut was a homemade green walnut liquor, brought out when someone suggested it might be a good match. Seven of the eight tasters chose the sherry again to pair with the force noire; the lone dissenter preferred the five-year-old Madeira. The ten-year-old Madeira and the port were also popular choices. Even though the confections, especially those made with dark chocolate, didn't taste especially sweet, they were sweeter than any dry wine, and that sweetness made the wine taste acidic and unpleasant. The fortified wines had a sweetness of their own that married nicely with the confections.

So, in addition to water, consider serving a good cream sherry at your chocolate party. If you want a broader selection, add a Marsala, a ruby port, and a Madeira.

In addition to water, consider serving a good cream sherry at your chocolate party. If you want a broader selection, add a Marsala, a ruby port, and a Madeira.

If your confection selection includes nut-filled chocolates or nut barks and you have access to walnut orchards, make a green walnut liquor following the recipe of Jack Mariani of Mariani Nut Company in Winters, California. His Croatian grandfather, who drank a small glass of the liquor before lunch and then another before retiring for the night and lived to be ninety-four, started the family tradition.

Jack Mariani's Green Walnut Liquor (Orahovica)

About 1 quart

8 green walnuts (available in the spring before the shells have hardened)
4 fresh orange leaves, if available
4 fresh lemon leaves, if available
1 quart inexpensive vodka
1½ cups (10½ ounces) granulated cane sugar
1 teaspoon pure vanilla extract, preferably Madagascar Bourbon

- Rinse the nuts well in cool water. Process the whole nuts, including the hulls, in a food processor until they are in ¼-inch chunks. Put them in a 2-quart glass jar. Add the leaves, vodka, sugar, and vanilla extract and stir together. Cover the top of the jar with cheesecloth. Put the jar in a sunny spot and leave it for 40 days and nights. The liquid will gradually turn a deep brown.

- Strain the liquid through a fine-mesh sieve into clean jars and cap tightly. It will keep in a cool, dark place for at least 1 year.

GLOSSARY, RESOURCES, BIBLIOGRAPHY, CONVERSION CHART & INDEX

GLOSSARY

Barley-malt syrup

Made by drying sprouted barley, mixing it with water, and then cooking it until it forms a syrup, barley-malt syrup has a distinct flavor that anyone who ate malted milk balls as a child will recognize. Because malt syrup is used in brewing, hops are sometimes added, which contribute bitterness, a flavor welcome in some beers but not in chocolate creations. Look for unhopped barley-malt syrup in health-food stores.

Butter

Use unsalted butter with 82% butterfat, such as Plugrá, Keller's, some Land O'Lakes products, and all unsalted European butters, in any recipe calling for butter in this book.

Chocolate bloom

A problem with the cocoa-butter crystals that results in a dull gray, white, or matte appearance on the surface or interior of chocolate. It is caused by poorly established tempering, cold cooling temperatures, or storage temperatures that are too warm or fluctuating.

Chocolate liquor

Cocoa nibs that have been ground into a paste. The processing combines the two components, cocoa solids and cocoa butter, of the roasted nibs.

Chocolate percentage

A number found on the labels of better chocolates that indicates the total percentage of cocoa solids and cocoa butter that the chocolate contains.

Cocoa beans

Also called cacao beans, these are the seeds inside the pods of the cacao tree that are processed to make chocolate.

Cocoa butter

Also called cacao butter, a complex fat in the cocoa bean that makes up about half its weight. It possesses four types of crystals with different melting points.

Cocoa-butter equivalents

Vegetable fats used to replace up to 5% of the cocoa butter in chocolate, a practice now allowed in England and Europe (much to the dismay of some chocolate makers and all lovers of good chocolate). In the United States, the only fat allowed other than cocoa butter is dairy butterfat. The amount must be lower than 12%, and the label must state that the chocolate contains butterfat.

Cocoa nibs

Bits of cocoa beans that have been roasted and shelled. They are the raw product that is made into finished chocolate, although they can be used on their own.

Cocoa powder

Cocoa liquor that has been pressed to remove most of the cocoa butter and is then ground to a fine powder. Sometimes the liquor is treated with an alkali solution that neutralizes the natural acids present. This treatment, called Dutching, was invented by the Dutch chemist Coenraad Johannes Van Houten in 1828. It makes the powder darker and milder. Today there are advocates of both types of cocoa powder, Dutch processed and natural.

Couverture

French for "coating," this term describes a finished chocolate particularly suited for dipping or molding because it contains more cocoa butter, at least 32%, making it less viscous. Virtually all of the higher-percentage chocolates fall into this category.

Cream

Many recipes in this book call for heavy whipping cream, which can vary considerably in fat content. A butterfat content in the higher range is desirable, but most packaging does not include a figure for butterfat. Check the nutritional content on cartons and buy cream that has at least 6 grams of fat per serving, which means that it has a butterfat content of just under 42%. Avoid cream that is ultrapasteurized or that contains sugar or flavorings.

Cream sherry

A fortified sweet Spanish wine with an alcohol content of at least 18%. The best cream sherries are made from Palomino grapes in the oloroso style, and are sweetened by the addition of wine made from the Pedro Ximénez grape, which is rich in natural sugars. Cream sherry is a good wine to serve with chocolate.

GLOSSARY (CONTINUED)

Dark or bittersweet chocolate

Chocolate with a percentage of chocolate liquor that ranges from 35% in standard chocolates to as much as 82% in the new chocolates.

Invert sugar

A stable sugar syrup made from sucrose that has been treated to break it down into its two simple sugars, glucose and fructose.

Lecithin

A soy-based emulsifier used in small quantities in the making of chocolate to yield a smoother and more fluid result.

Madeira

A robust fortified wine made on the Atlantic island of Madeira, situated off the Portuguese mainland. Those made from either Bual or Malmsey grapes and labeled either Reserve or Special Reserve are good choices for serving with chocolates.

Marsala

A fortified wine from Sicily that ranges from dry to sweet. Look for bottles labeled Fine and Sweet to pair with chocolates.

Milk chocolate

Chocolate with a minimum of 10% chocolate liquor and 12% milk solids, although the new chocolates contain as much as 41% chocolate liquor.

Port

A brandy-fortified red wine named after Oporto, Portugal. Ruby ports are aged two or three years, while tawny ports are aged, usually in wood, for a longer time. Either one pairs with chocolate.

Semisweet chocolate

Chocolate that contains at least 15% chocolate liquor by weight. This term is rarely used to describe the new chocolates.

Sugar bloom

An accumulation of sugar crystals on the surface of chocolate brought on by too moist an environment.

Tempered chocolate

Chocolate that has been heated and then cooled to specific temperatures so that the fat fractions in the cocoa butter crystallize properly, resulting in a high sheen.

Unsweetened chocolate

Chocolate liquor without added sugar.

Vanilla

Vanilla is the pod fruit of a climbing orchid plant. Growing the plant and curing the pods are both labor-intensive, factors that account for vanilla's high price in the market. Both whole pods and an extract made from them are used in this book. Tahitian beans are frequently called for because they are very fruity and floral, qualities that go well with chocolate. Madagascar Bourbon extract has a strong vanilla aroma and is preferred in recipes that benefit from that quality.

White chocolate

Chocolate that contains not less than 20% cocoa fat, 3½% milk fat, and 14% total milk solids, as well as not more than 55% sweetener.

Resources

American Chocolate Designs

www.americanchocolatedesigns.com

877-442-3682

Transfer sheets of every description, including custom designs, are available here, although the minimum order of a single design is twenty-five sheets.

Barry-Callebaut

www.barry-callebaut.com

Learn about this large chocolate company, including its chocolate academy, at this site.

Chocosphere

www.chocosphere.com

877-992-4626

Chocosphere has a wide array of chocolates, including El Rey (including nibs), the E. Guittard line, Valrhona, Callebaut, Scharffen Berger, Michel Cluizel, Lindt, and others.

Chocovision

www.chocovision.com

880-324-6252

This is a good source for small tempering machines, as well as Callebaut, Guittard, and Scharffen Berger chocolates.

E. Dehillerin

18-20, rue Coquillière

75001 Paris, France

01.42.36.53.13

This is a cookware paradise, including a large selection of chocolate molds. Many of the salespeople speak English.

El Rey Chocolates

www.elreychocolates.com

800-357-3999

Here is Venezuelan chocolate, as well as cocoa nibs, from the source.

Gourmail

www.gourmail.com

800-366-5900

This company carries Callebaut, Cacao Barry, Valrhona, and El Rey chocolates.

Guittard Chocolate Company

www.guittard.com

800-468-2462

Guittard is a family-owned company south of San Francisco established not long after the California gold rush. Its new line, which includes higher-percentage chocolates and single-bean varietals, is available on this site. Cocoa nibs are also available.

Hilliard's Chocolate Systems

http://209.25.139.27

800-258-1530

Hilliard manufactures equipment for the chocolate trade, including the Little Dipper, a tempering machine suitable for home use.

J.B. Prince Company

www.jbprince.com

800-473-0577

This New York–based source carries very reasonably priced chocolate molds and tempering machines in three styles. There is a fifty-dollar minimum order for U.S. delivery.

Kerekes

www.bakedeco.com

800-525-5556

Here's a site with a good choice of chocolate molds and transfer sheets.

Kitchen Krafts

www.kitchenkrafts.com

800-776-0575

This site has invert sugar (Nulomoline).

La Cuisine

www.lacuisineus.com

800-521-1176

La Cuisine is a retail store in Alexandria, Virginia, with a Web site that sells chocolate molds, sugar pots, and transfer sheets, as well as Michel Cluizel, Valrhona, and other chocolates.

Leaves Pure Teas

www.leaves.com

877-532-8378

Leaves is a high-quality source for teas for ganaches.

Melissa's

www.melissas.com

800-588-0151

Melissa's, a large company specializing in international produce, carries fresh Key limes.

M.O.R.A.

13, rue Montmartre

75001 Paris, France

01.45.08.19.24

Bakers and confectioners will find everything they need here, including many molds and pans not seen in the United States.

Nielsen-Massey Vanillas, Inc.

www.nielsenmassey.com

800-525-7873

This company is a great source for vanilla beans and pure vanilla extract, including Madagascar Bourbon, Tahitian, and Mexican.

Pastry Chef Central

www.pastrychef.com

561-999-9483

Belgian chocolate molds are available through this site.

Penzey's Spices

www.penzeys.com

800-741-7787

A popular spice house with a large inventory, Penzey's carries decorticated cardamom.

Prévin, Incorporated

www.previninc.com

215-985-0323

Prévin is a restaurant-supply store in Philadelphia that has a good selection of chocolate molds.

Pure Spice

www.purespice.com

866-532-1703

Pure Spice is another source for decorticated cardamom.

Scharffen Berger Chocolate Maker

www.scharffenberger.com

800-930-4528

This small artisanal company started making high-quality, higher-percentage chocolates near San Francisco in 1997. Their chocolates, including cocoa nibs, are available at this site.

Simplers Botanical Company

www.simplers.com

800-652-7646

This company produces essential oils, including rose geranium, lavender, and lemon verbena. Their oils are also available at many health-foods stores.

SugarCraft

www.sugarcraft.com

SugarCraft is another source of invert sugar (Nulomoline).

Sur La Table

www.surlatable.com

866-328-5412

This source has sheet pans, baking pans, crystallized ginger, Microplane graters, thermometers, scales, and other baking equipment, available on the Internet, by catalog, or in their more than fifty retail stores in the United States. The stores carry Scharffen Berger and Michel Cluizel chocolate.

Sweet Celebrations, Inc. (formally Maid of Scandinavia)

www.sweetc.com

800-328-6722

In addition to an array of equipment for the home baker, this site carries invert sugar (Nulomoline) and Valrhona, Callebaut, and Lindt chocolates.

The Vanilla Company

www.vanilla.com

800-757-7511

This is a source for all things vanilla, including whole beans and pure extracts.

Village Imports

www.levillage.com

888-873-7194

Small bars of a wide range of Valrhona chocolates are available here. Call for larger quantities.

Whole Foods Markets

These upscale grocery stores have more than one hundred locations in the United States. Although stock in individual stores varies, many carry Callebaut, El Rey, and Scharffen Berger chocolates cut from professional-sized bars and sold by the pound.

Williams Sonoma

www.williams-sonoma.com

877-812-6235

This is a good source for candy makers and bakers, carrying a full line of supplies available at two hundred retail stores, online, and through a catalog. Valrhona and Scharffen Berger chocolates are available in the stores.

Zingerman's

www.zingermans.com

888-636-8162

This Midwest specialty store carries Valrhona, El Rey, Michel Cluizel, and Scharffen Berger chocolates in small bars that are handy for taste testing before buying larger quantities.

Other Resources

Local candy-making supply stores and stores selling art supplies carry many of the things you might need, including plain acetate squares to use for decorating dipped chocolates and 23-karat gold leaf in sheets.

Bibliography

Alikonis, Justin J. *Candy Technology*. Westport, Connecticut: AVI Publishing Co., Inc, 1979.

Bau, Fréderic. *Au coeur des saveurs*. Barcelona: Montagud Editores, S.A., 1998.

Campbell, Dawn L. *The Tea Book*. Gretna, Louisiana: Pelican Publishing Company, 1995.

Charley, Helen, and Connie Weaver. *Foods: A Scientific Approach*. 3rd ed. Upper Saddle River, New Jersey: Prentice-Hall, Inc., 1998.

Coe, Sophie D., and Michael D. Coe. *The True History of Chocolate*. London: Thames and Hudson, Ltd., 1996.

Corriher, Shirley O. *Cookwise*. New York: William Morrow, 1997.

Dand, Robin. *The International Cocoa Trade*. Cambridge: Woodhead Publishing Limited, 1999.

Davidson, Alan. *The Oxford Companion to Food*. Oxford: Oxford University Press, 1999.

Friedrich, Jacqueline. *A Wine and Food Guide to the Loire*. New York: Henry Holt and Company, 1996.

González, Elaine. *The Art of Chocolate*. San Francisco: Chronicle Books, 1998.

Greenspan, Dorie. *Chocolate Desserts by Pierre Hermé*. New York: Little, Brown and Company, 2001.

Kourik, Robert. *The Lavender Garden*. San Francisco: Chronicle Books, 1998.

Kummer, Corby. "Where Chocolate Grows on Trees." *The Atlantic Monthly* (October 1995): 110–113.

Lees, R., and E.B. Jackson. *Sugar Confectionery and Chocolate Manufacture*. Glasgow, UK: Blackie Academic & Professional, 1994.

McGee, Harold. *On Food and Cooking*. rev. ed. New York: Scribner, 2004.

Medrich, Alice. *Bittersweet*. New York: Artisan, 2003.

Presilla, Maricel E. *The New Taste of Chocolate*. Berkekey: Ten Speed Press, 2001.

Richart, Michel. *Chocolat mon amour*. Paris: Somogy Editions d'art, 2001.

Robinson, Jancis. *The Oxford Companion to Wine*. Oxford: Oxford University Press, 1994.

Schneider, Elizabeth. "Where the Chocolate Tree Blooms." *Saveur* (September/October 1995): 96–106.

Trager, James. *The Food Chronology*. New York: Henry Holt, 1995.

Conversion Chart

VOLUME EQUIVALENTS

These are not exact equivalents for American cups and spoons,
but have been rounded up or down slightly to make measuring easier.

American	Metric	Imperial
¼ t	1.2 ml	
½ t	2.5 ml	
1 t	5.0 ml	
½ T (1.5 t)	7.5 ml	
1 T (3 t)	15 ml	
¼ cup (4 T)	60 ml	2 fl oz
⅓ cup (5 T)	75 ml	2½ fl oz
½ cup (8 T)	125 ml	4 fl oz
⅔ cup (10 T)	150 ml	5 fl oz
¾ cup (12 T)	175 ml	6 fl oz
1 cup (16 T)	250 ml	8 fl oz
1¼ cups	300 ml	10 fl oz (½ pt)
1½ cups	350 ml	12 fl oz
2 cups (1 pint)	500 ml	16 fl oz
2½ cups	625 ml	20 fl oz (1 pint)
1 quart	1 liter	32 fl oz

OVEN TEMPERATURE EQUIVALENTS

Oven Mark	F	C	Gas
Very cool	250–275	130–140	½–1
Cool	300	150	2
Warm	325	170	3
Moderate	350	180	4
Moderately hot	375	190	5
	400	200	6
Hot	425	220	7
	450	230	8
Very hot	475	250	9

WEIGHT EQUIVALENTS

The metric weights given in this chart are not exact equivalents,
but have been rounded up or down slightly to make measuring easier.

Avoirdupois	Metric
¼ oz	7 g
½ oz	15 g
1 oz	28 g
2 oz	60 g
3 oz	90 g
4 oz	115 g
5 oz	150 g
6 oz	175 g
7 oz	200 g
8 oz (½ lb)	225 g
9 oz	250 g
10 oz	300 g
11 oz	325 g
12 oz	350 g
13 oz	375 g
14 oz	400 g
15 oz	425 g
16 oz (1 lb)	454 g
1½ lb	750 g
2 lb	900 g
2¼ lb	1 kg
3 lb	1.4 kg
4 lb	1.8 kg

Index

Page numbers in *italic* denote photographs

A

Acetate squares, decorating with, *32–33*, 34
Almonds:
    chocolate and nut butter filling, 89
    chocolate-covered caramelized, 119

B

Banana, roasted, ice cream, 169
Barks, *132*, 133–141
    caramelized cocoa nib white chocolate,
        140, *141*
    caramelized peanut milk chocolate, 138–39
    dark chocolate
      cashew-sesame, 134
      dried-fruit, 135
      extra-bitter, candied orange peel, 137
      hazelnut, pumpkin seed, and pistachio,
        136, *136*
Brittle, honeycomb, malt ganache with,
      76–77, *77*
Brownie(s):
    fudge, 99
    ice-cream sandwiches, 104–5
    rocky Recchiuti, *100*, 101
Burnt caramel, 149
    base, 70
    correct hue for, *71*
    ganache, 72–73
    ice cream, 166
    milk chocolate with, drink, 148, *148*
    pots de crème, 126, *127*
    sauce, 156
Buttermilk–Meyer lemon ice cream, 168, *168*

C

Cacao tree, 14
Cakes. *See* Cupcakes
Candied:
    citrus peel, 114–15
    grapefruit, tarragon ganache with, 62–63

orange peel extra-bitter chocolate bark, 137
Caramel(s):
    burnt, 149
    base, 70
    correct hue for, *71*
    ganache, 72–73
    ice cream, 166
    milk chocolate with, drink, 148, *148*
    pots de crème, 126, *127*
    sauce, 156
    fleur de sel, 78–79
    rose, filling, 82–83, *83*
Caramelization, sugar cooked to
    three stages of, *71*
Caramelized:
    cashews, chocolate-covered, 118–19
    cocoa nib(s)
      ice cream with, 170, *171*
      white chocolate bark, 140, *141*
    ganache with sesame nougat, 74–75
    hazelnuts, chocolate-covered, 117–18
    peanut milk chocolate bark, 138–39
Cardamom ganache with cardamom nougat,
    64–65
Cashew(s):
    chocolate-covered caramelized, 118–19
    sesame dark chocolate bark, 134
Chai, milk chocolate, 150
Chocolate(s):
    choosing, 17
    making of, 14–15
    new, 15–16
    organizing work with, 18–19
    storing, 16
    tempering, 28–29
Chocolate liquor, 14, 15
Chocolate percentage, 15–16
Chocolate-tasting party, 175–79
Citrus peel, candied, 114–15
Le Club du Chocolat aux Palais, 130–31
Cluizel, Michel, 15
Cocoa beans, 14

Cocoa nib(s), 14
    caramelized, white chocolate bark, 140, *141*
    ice cream with caramelized cocoa nibs, 170, *171*
    topping, two-chocolate ganache with, 58–59
Coffee:
    espresso, white chocolate topping (for cupcakes),
        121
    Kona, ganache, 84–85, *85*
    white chocolate mocha drink, 152, *153*
Colombian chocolate:
    malt ice cream, 167
    varietal chocolate ganache, 68–69
Confections, 27–91
    fleur de sel caramels, 78–79
    organizing work for, 18–19
    tempering chocolate for, 28–29
    see also Dipped chocolates; Ganache(s); Molded
        chocolates; Truffles
Cookies:
    chocolate-dipped sesame *tuiles*, 110–11, *111*
    chocolate shortbread, with truffle cream filling,
        106, 107–8
    triple-chocolate, 109
Cupcakes:
    devil's food, with white chocolate–espresso
        topping, 121
    gingerbread, with white chocolate–lemon topping,
        124–25
    white, with truffle cream topping,
        122–23, *123*

D
Dark chocolate:
    bark
        cashew-sesame, 134
        dried-fruit, 135
        hazelnut, pumpkin seed, and pistachio,
            136, *136*
    chocolate percentage in, 15–16
    double, soufflés, *127*, 128–29
    making of, 14–15
    mint drink, 146

recipe testing and, 16
    sauces
        malt, 158
        orange, 157
    varietal, drink, 147
Decorating:
    dipped chocolates, *32–33*, 33–34, *35*
    molded chocolates, 39
Devil's food cupcakes with white chocolate–espresso
        topping, 121
Dipped chocolates:
    decorating tops of, *32–33*, 33–34, *35*
    dipping technique for, *30*, 31
    fleur de sel caramels, 78–79
    ganaches for, 45–77. *See also* Ganache(s)
    storing, 31
    tempering chocolate for, 28–29
Double–dark chocolate soufflés, *128*, 128–29
Dried-fruit:
    clusters, 113
    dark chocolate bark, 135
Drinks, 145–53
    dark chocolate
        mint, 146
        varietal, 147
    green walnut liquor (orahovica), Jack Mariani's,
        179
    milk chocolate
        with burnt caramel, 148, *148*
        chai, 150
        malt, 151
    pairing with chocolate, 177–78
    white chocolate mocha, 152, *153*

E
Earl Grey tea ganache, 46–47
Eatwell Farm, Dixon, Calif., 162–63
Equipment, 21–23
Espresso:
    white chocolate mocha drink, 152, *153*
    white chocolate topping (for cupcakes),
        121

Extra-bitter chocolate:
    bark, candied orange peel, 137
    sauce, 159

F
Farmers' market (San Francisco), 92–93
Fillings:
    for molded confections, 17, 81
        chocolate and nut butter, 89–90, *91*
        ginger ganache, 86–87
        Kona coffee ganache, 84–85, *85*
        rose caramel, 82–83, *83*
        star anise–pink peppercorn ganache, 87–88
        truffle cream, *106*, 107–8
Fleur de sel caramels, 78–79
Force noire ganache, 54–55, *55*
Fudge brownies, 99

G
Ganache(s):
    burnt caramel, 72–73
    caramelized, with sesame nougat, 74–75
    cutting into 1-inch squares, 31
    dipping into chocolate, 31
    fillings for molded chocolates
        ginger, 86–87
        Kona coffee, 84–85, *85*
        star anise–pink peppercorn, 87–88
    infused, 42–65
        cardamom, with cardamom nougat, 64–65
        Earl Grey tea, 46–47
        force noire, 54–55, *55*
        jasmine tea, 48–49
        lavender vanilla, 56–57
        lemon verbena, 60–61
        mint tea, 50–51
        tarragon, with candied grapefruit, 62–63
        with tea, 43, 45–51
        tips for, 42–43
        two-chocolate, with cocoa nib topping, 58–59
    making, 40–42
    malt, with honeycomb brittle, 76–77, *77*

new higher-percentage chocolates and, 15–16
    organizing work for, 18–19
    rolling into truffles, 37
    trimmings, turning into truffles, 37
    varietal chocolate, 68–69
Gingerbread cupcakes with white chocolate–
    lemon topping, 124–25
Ginger ganache, 86–87
Graham crackers, 96
    s'mores, 98
Grapefruit peel, candied, 114–15
    tarragon ganache with, 62–63
Green walnut liquor (orahovica), Jack Mariani's,
    179

H
Hazelnut(s):
    chocolate and nut butter filling, 89–90, *91*
    chocolate-covered caramelized, 117–18
    pumpkin seed, and pistachio dark chocolate
        bark, 136, *136*
Honeycomb brittle, malt ganache with,
    76–77, *77*
    Horlick, William, 151

I
Ice creams, 165–73
    burnt caramel, 166
    cocoa nib, with caramelized cocoa nibs,
        170, *171*
    Colombian chocolate malt, 167
    Meyer lemon–buttermilk, 168, *168*
    roasted banana, 169
    vanilla bean, 172, *173*
Ice-cream sandwiches:
    brownie, 104–5
    classic, 102–103
Infused ganaches. See Ganache(s)–infused
Invert sugar, 42

J
Jasmine tea ganache, 48–49

K

Key lime pears, 112–13
Kona coffee ganache, 84–85, *85*

L

Lavender:
    farming, 162–63
    vanilla ganache, 56–57
Lemon:
    Meyer, buttermilk ice cream, 168, *168*
    white chocolate topping (for cupcakes), 124–25
Lemon verbena ganache, 60–61
Lime, Key, pears, 112–13

M

Malt:
    Colombian chocolate ice cream, 167
    dark chocolate sauce, 158
    ganache with honeycomb brittle, 76–77, *77*
    milk chocolate drink, 151
Mariani, Jack, 179
Markings, decorative, on dipped chocolates, *32–33*,
        34, *35*
Marshmallows:
    rocky Recchiuti brownies, *100*, 101
    s'mores, 98
    Tahitian vanilla bean, 97–98
Measurements, 23
Meyer lemon–buttermilk ice cream, 168, *168*
Milk chocolate:
    bark, caramelized peanut, 138–39
    with burnt caramel drink, 148, *148*
    caramelized ganache with sesame nougat,
        74–75
    chai, 150
    chocolate percentage in, 15, 16
    making of, 14, 15
    malt drink, 151
    and nut butter filling, 89–90, *91*
    peanut butter pucks, 116
    recipe testing and, 16
    sauce, 158

Mint:
    dark chocolate drink, 146
    tea ganache, 50–51
Mocha drink, white chocolate, 152, *153*
Molded chocolates, *38*, 39–40, *41*, 81–91
    fillings for, 17, 81
        chocolate and nut butter, 89–90, *91*
        ginger ganache, 86–87
        Kona coffee ganache, 84–85, *85*
        rose caramel, 82–83, *83*
        star anise–pink peppercorn ganache, 87–88
    making, 39–40
    organizing work for, 18–19
    tempering chocolate for, 28–29
Molds, chocolate, 39
Monteaux, Danielle, 130–31

N

Nougat:
    cardamom, cardamom ganache with, 64–65
    sesame, caramelized ganache with, 74–75
Nut butter(s):
    and chocolate filling, 89–90, *91*
    peanut butter pucks, 116

O

Orahovica (green walnut liquor), Jack Mariani's, 179
Orange:
    dark chocolate sauce, 157
    peel, candied, 114–15
        extra-bitter chocolate bark, 137

P

Paris, chocolate clubs in, 130–31
Peanut:
    butter pucks, 116
    caramelized, milk chocolate bark, 138–39
Pears, Key lime, 112–13
Peppercorn, pink, star anise ganache, 87–88
Pink peppercorn–star anise ganache, 87–88
Pistachio, hazelnut, and pumpkin seed dark chocolate
        bark, 136, *136*

Pots de crème, burnt caramel, 126, *127*
Pumpkin seed, hazelnut, and pistachio dark chocolate bark, 136, *136*

R
Raspberry white chocolate sauce with thyme, 160, *161*
Recchiuti Confections, 24–25, 92–93
Rose caramel filling, 82–83, *83*

S
Sauces, 155–61
    burnt caramel, 156
    dark chocolate
        extra-bitter, 159
        malt, 158
        orange, 157
    milk chocolate, 158
    raspberry white chocolate, with thyme, 160, *161*
"Seed" method, 28–29
Sesame:
    cashew dark chocolate bark, 134
    nougat, caramelized ganache with, 74–75
    tuiles, chocolate-dipped, 110–11, *111*
Shortbread cookies, chocolate, with truffle cream filling, *106*, 107–8
S'mores, 98
Snacks, 95–129
    brownies
        fudge, 99
        rocky Recchiuti, *100*, 101
    burnt caramel pots de crème, 126, *127*
    candied citrus peel, 114–15
    chocolate-covered caramelized nuts
        cashews, 118–19
        hazelnuts, 117–18
    cookies
        chocolate-dipped sesame *tuiles*, 110–11, *111*
        chocolate shortbread, with truffle cream filling, *106*, 107–8
        triple-chocolate, 109

cupcakes
    devil's food, with white chocolate–espresso topping, 121
    gingerbread, with white chocolate–lemon topping, 124–25
    white, with truffle cream topping, 122–23, *123*
double–dark chocolate soufflés, *128*, 128–29
dried-fruit clusters, 113
graham crackers, 96
ice-cream sandwiches
    brownie, 104–5
    classic, 102–103
Key lime pears, 112–13
peanut butter pucks, 116
s'mores, 98
Tahitian vanilla bean marshmallows, 97–98
whoopie pies, 120
Soufflés, double–dark chocolate, *128*, 128–29
Star anise–pink peppercorn ganache, 87–88
Sugar:
    cooked to three stages of caramelization, *71*
    invert, 42
    see also Caramel(s)

T
Tahitian vanilla bean marshmallows, 97–98
Tarragon ganache with candied grapefruit, 62–63
Tasting chocolate, 17
    chocolate-tasting party, 175–79
    at Le Club du Chocolat aux Palais in Paris, 130–31
Tea:
    ganaches infused with, 43, 45–51
        Earl Grey, 46–47
        jasmine, 48–49
        mint, 50–51
    milk chocolate chai, 150
Tempering chocolate, 28–29
Testing recipes, 16, 143
Thyme, raspberry white chocolate sauce with, 160, *161*

Tools, 21–23
Toppings:
    for cupcakes
        truffle cream, 122–23, *123*
        white chocolate–espresso, 121
        white chocolate–lemon, 124–25
        decorative, on dipped chocolates, 34, *35*
Triple-chocolate cookies, 109
Truffle cream:
    filling, chocolate shortbread cookies with, *106*,
        107–8
    topping (for cupcakes), 122–23, *123*
Truffles, *36*
    ganaches for, 45–73. *See also* Ganache(s)
    rolling ganache into, 37
    turning ganache trimmings into, 37
Tuiles, sesame, chocolate-dipped, 110–11, *111*
Two-chocolate ganache with cocoa nib topping,
        58–59

V
Vanilla:
    bean
        ice cream, 172, *173*
        Tahitian, marshmallows, 97–98
    lavender ganache, 56–57

Varietal chocolate, 15
    dark, drink, 147
    ganache, 68–69

W
Walnut(s):
    green, liquor (orahovica), Jack Mariani's, 179
    rocky Recchiuti brownies, *100*, 101
Weather, working with chocolate and, 18
Weights and measures, 23
White chocolate:
    bark, caramelized cocoa nib, 140, *141*
    espresso topping (for cupcakes), 121
    lemon topping (for cupcakes), 124–25
    making of, 14, 15
    malt ganache with honeycomb brittle, 76–77, *77*
    mocha drink, 152, *153*
    molded chocolates
        with ginger ganache, 86–87
        with rose caramel filling, 82–83, *83*
    raspberry sauce with thyme, 160, *161*
    recipe testing and, 16
White cupcakes with truffle cream topping, 122–23,
        123
Whoopie pies, 120
Wines, pairing with chocolate, 177–78